Learning in doing: Social, cognitive, and computational
perspectives

GENERAL EDITORS: ROY PEA
                  JOHN SEELEY BROWN

The construction zone: Working for cognitive change in school

The construction zone
Working for cognitive change in school

DENIS NEWMAN
PEG GRIFFIN
MICHAEL COLE

With the collaboration of
SHELIA BROYLES
ANDREA L. PETITTO
MARILYN G. QUINSAAT

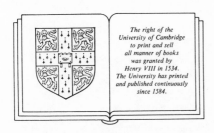

The right of the
University of Cambridge
to print and sell
all manner of books
was granted by
Henry VIII in 1534.
The University has printed
and published continuously
since 1584.

CAMBRIDGE UNIVERSITY PRESS
Cambridge
New York   New Rochelle
Melbourne   Sydney

Published by the Press Syndicate of the University of Cambridge
The Pitt Building, Trumpington Street, Cambridge CB2 1RP
32 East 57th Street, New York, NY 10022, USA
10 Stamford Road, Oakleigh, Melbourne 3166, Australia

First published 1989

Printed in the United States of America

Library of Congress Cataloging in Publication Data
Newman, Denis.
The construction zone.
(Learning in doing: social, cognitive, and computational perspectives)
1. Learning, Psychology of. 2. Cognition in children. 3. Child
development. 4. Social interaction in children. I. Griffin, Peg.
II. Cole, Michael. III. Title. IV. Series: Learning in doing.
LB1060.N49 1989 370.15′2 88-20369

British Library Cataloguing in Publication Data
Newman, Denis
The construction zone: working for cognitive change in school.
(Learning in doing: social, cognitive, and computational perspectives).
1. Primary schools students. Cognitive development
1. Title II. Griffin, Peg III. Cole, Michael, *1938–*
IV. Series
370.15′2

ISBN 0–521–36266–0 hard covers
ISBN 0–521–38942–9 paperback

Contents

Series foreword

The *situated* nature of learning, remembering, and understanding is a central fact. It may appear obvious that human minds develop in social situations, and that they use the tools and representational media that culture provides to support, extend, and reorganize mental functioning. But cognitive theories of knowledge representation and educational practice, in school and in the workplace, have not been sufficiently responsive to questions about these relationships. And the need for responsiveness has become salient as computational media radically reshape the frontiers of individual and social action, and as educational achievement fails to translate into effective use of knowledge.

This series is born of the conviction that new and exciting interdisciplinary syntheses are under way, as scholars and practitioners from diverse fields seek to analyze and influence the new transformations of social and mental life, and to understand successful learning wherever it occurs.

Computational media include not only computers but the vast array of expressive, receptive, and presentational devices available for use with computers, including interactive video, optical media such as CD-ROM and CD-I, networks, hypermedia systems, workgroup collaboration tools, speech recognition and synthesis, image processing and animation, and software more generally.

These technologies are dramatically transforming the basic patterns of communication and knowledge interchange in societies, and automating the component processes of thinking and problem-solving. In changing situations of knowledge acquisition and use, the new interactive technologies redefine – in ways yet to be determined –

what it means to know and understand, and what it means to become "literate" or an "educated citizen."

The series invites contributions that advance our understanding of these seminal issues.

Foreword

This book gives some powerful insights about what goes on when teachers teach and pupils learn, and about the chemistry – or better, the alchemy – of human cooperation. The book introduces the reader to the "construction zone," a magic place where minds meet, where things are not the same to all who see them, where meanings are fluid, and where one person's construal may preempt another's.

For students, the book is a case study in creative research – work going beyond the squared-off, hypothesis-testing studies favored by the journals. The authors begin by trying to establish a much-talked-about imaginary: the same task in different settings.

What does it mean, in terms of the methodology upon which an assessment of cognitive processes is based, to say that you have *the same task in different settings?* And if you don't know how to identify "same tasks," what is the basis for your judgment that some children perform well in one version of "the" task and not another? (p. 11)

The imaginary has only been glimpsed, so to speak, over the shoulder. People interested in culture and context always talk as though some imaginary equalization has or has not existed in some past study or school setting. Can one, deliberately and concretely, establish the same task in different situations? It turns out, in the end, that one can do so only in a weak and unpersuasive way. The authors pursue this legend with an intelligent, stubborn inquiry. They are able, finally, to turn away from the question with which they began and to move to a position from which the originating question dissolves. What we usually talk about as a task, they conclude, is not a real thing. It is a strategic fiction, a blueprint, a scheme used to help people interorganize their activities.

Students ought to look at living, moving, thoughtful research like this. These are not pretty studies, but there is intellectual excitement in this book. Sometimes one worries whether the escalating routines and rituals defining well-formed studies may perfect research to death.

The substantive work of the book presents a challenge to our traditional view of learning, a challenge that is straightforward, fundamental, and much needed. Beginning with William James, American psychologists have thought about adaptation in all its forms – learning, cognitive change, cognitive development – as something that takes place in individuals. Behind the scenes, there have been struggles. Some have argued that the individual's qualities only exist in group life. John Dewey (1922) said that habits are social functions. In *Human Nature and Conduct*, subtitled *An Introduction to Social Psychology*, he said:

> Honesty, chastity, malice, peevishness, courage, triviality, industry, irresponsibility are not private possessions of a person. They are working adaptations of personal capacities with environing forces. All virtues and vices are habits which incorporate objective forces.

Some people – Wundt, McDougall, Durkheim, Halbwachs – went further than Dewey was willing to go, saying that groups actually think, proposing theoretical entities such as group minds, collective memories, and folk psychologies. Americans stoutly resisted both the psychologizing of the group and the sociologizing of the individual. Americans formed an experimental social psychology in which individuals and groups were clearly, perhaps too clearly, differentiated.

What Newman, Griffin, and Cole call a false dichotomy arose – the individual on the one side, the directive, persuasive, or coercive force of the group on the other. The individual has freestanding habits, attitudes, knowledge, intellectual structure, and cognitive processes. Other individuals, no less freestanding and well-bounded, provide stimuli, tell, instruct, transmit, indoctrinate. The very description seems to set the stage for a struggle. Who is to be active, who passive? Who ought to control the flow of the learning? Should teachers teach or should students discover?

One of the fundamental insights leading to this work was the recognition of what the authors call indeterminacy of discourse. Utterances may have multiple functions. They may transmit information while at the same time managing and modifying the social situation in which the conversation takes place. Furthermore, communication does not have to be exact in order to bring people together. People go along with one another. They sustain conversations without full communication or completely clear understandings, trying to work out in the course of the speech what the other might mean.

The situation is one that college instructors are familiar with. The instructor is trying to establish a classroom discussion, and a student stands up and asks a question that doesn't make sense or that seems obviously shallow and uncomprehending. Classroom discussion is a fragile flower. "Dumb" questions test an instructor's mind and intentions. Students watch to see how the instructor will respond, and the instructor knows they do. He wants to give a question the weight it deserves, but he doesn't want to cut the questioner down. So he probes, leading the student into discussion, trying to move from the original question toward other questions that are more worth discussion, more answerable, or both. Sometimes the instructor discovers what the student had in mind in the first place. Sometimes the instructor and the questioner together find a reasonable question that can be addressed and answered with dignity and intellectual profit to both sides.

The instructor and the student have engaged for a short time in an indeterminate discourse. Maintaining conversation, they have sought a common ground of comprehension and understanding. For a few moments, the instructor has established what Vygotsky calls a zone of proximal development and what Newman, Griffin, and Cole call the construction zone. The construction zone mediates between the thought of two people. It is a shared activity in which interpsychological processes can take place.

Imagine, if you like, two people whose activities are linked together following relatively simple rhythms, routines, and prompts. The low-level cues sustain the activity, though the meanings and understandings possessed by each actor may be quite different. Through such shared activity a teacher may create (in Courtney Cazden's phrase) "competence before performance" or a zone of proximal development (ZPD). The shared activity does not necessarily mean a completely shared understanding of the meaning of the activity, or of each other:

Within a ZPD, objects do not have a unique analysis. An object such as a poem, a chart or a spoken concept may be understood very differently by the child and by the teacher. Likewise, the same speech act may be interpreted quite differently. But, these differences need not cause "trouble" for the teacher or the child or the social interaction; the participants can act as if their understandings are the same. At first, this systematic vagueness about what an object "really is" may appear to make cognitive analysis impossible. However, it now appears to us that this looseness is just what is needed to allow change to happen when people with differing analyses interact. It is also the key element for the process we call "appropriation." (p. 12)

The zone of proximal development is something more than the social support that some today call scaffolding; it is not just a set of devices used by one person to support high-level activity by another.

The ZPD is the locus of social negotiations about meanings, and it is, in the context of schools, a place where teachers and pupils may appropriate one another's understandings. Appropriation – Leont'ev's term – is in a formal sense the sociohistorical equivalent of the biologically based term assimilation. The teacher and pupil acting together may bring about a meeting of the minds. One of the more compelling things about the Newman, Griffin, and Cole formulation is that it brings, at last, into our talk about instruction that slight aura of fuzziness and confusion that is always a backdrop to real communication among people. Teachers and pupils need not understand one another much more than people generally do, or attain extraordinary precision of communication, to maintain a worthwhile educational process.

Just as the children do not have to know the full cultural analysis of a tool to begin using it, the teacher does not have to have a complete analysis of the children's understanding of the situation to start using their actions in the larger system." (p. 63)

How do the teacher and the child meet one another in the construction zone? The book provides some interesting examples.

• A frequent interpsychological activity in schools is an "Initiation, Response, Evaluation" or "Question, Answer, Feedback" sequence. The teacher initiates a topic; a child in the classroom proposes a completion or an answer; the teacher disposes of the child's response, affirming or negating it, usually in the act of initiating another topic. A series of three-part assertions runs together to form an instructional dialogue between a teacher and a classroom group. Newman, Griffin, and Cole argue that each three-part assertion may be seen as one assertion, collaboratively constructed by the teacher and the children. Actions of the teachers and pupils intermingle information, feedback, and social management. In an interesting sociopsychological analysis, the authors point out that this stereotyped instructional sequence works much better for children who represent the subject matter categorically rather than functionally. Observed "developmental shifts" from thematic to categorical conceptualization, commonly found when children enter school, may reflect the immersion of the children in interpsychological activities that selectively engage this kind of conceptualization and favor it.

• A teacher is teaching division to a class divided into five ability groups. The teacher begins with the assumption that an Extended Precision Procedure will guide all children to a solution, but she assumes that she will modify the procedure – choose an easier or harder elaboration – for children of different ability, and she does. Working with one child at a time, she steps the child through one of three or four solution processes. She varies the path to solution in part according to a child's formal grouping, in part according to her own estimation of what the child can cope with. The teaching of division is commonly described as a case of cut-and-dried procedural teaching and learning. One might diagram what the teacher is doing as a universally applied Extended Precision Procedure, but what happens isn't uniform. It is a mutual creation of a shared learning experience, and that interpsychological construction can be observed and studied.

Our analysis of the actual process of instruction of the division algorithm illustrates the idea that there are processes which must properly be characterized as interpsychological – arising from the interaction between people – which play a major role in producing cognitive changes. These interactive processes are accessible to observation and can provide an important link to explain cognitive change. (pp. 92–3)

In the last chapter of the book, "Conclusions for a Cognitive Science of Education," the authors come up with the interesting idea that what we generally call a task is not a real thing. It is an ideal, a template, a map that one follows to create a temporally organized sequence of behavior.

A cognitive science of education, which concerns the variety of settings in which cognitive change occurs, will have to think of tasks in a different way. We suggest that tasks are strategic fictions that people negotiate and use as a way of negotiating an intepretation of a situation. They are used by psychologists and teachers as well as children to help organize working together. (p. 135)

The achievement of this book is to mix some intriguing Vygotskian ideas with a creative research program to find ways to observe people moving towards shared understandings of the world – mechanisms mediating Berger and Luckmann's "social construction of reality."

We have had a limited armamentarium for observing and thinking about human learning; consequently, we tend to attribute the phenomena of learning to relatively simple, building-block mechanisms. Thinking about learning in this way, we are virtually forced to strategize about education through schemes of decomposition and reconstruction, to break apart the stream of human activity – into skills, schemes, behaviors, rule systems, subroutines, procedures – and then recompose a more sophisticated system. We are virtually forced into pedanticism. We move the would-be learner out of the complex, dynamic life of everyday activities and sit him or her down in front of workbooks, drill-and-practice exercises on vocabulary and multiplication, finger exercises, problem sets, reinforcement schedules, and so forth, and then try to build new skills and habits. Then, carefully, we try to find a way to reinsert both the learner and learning back into the real world.

Newman, Griffin, and Cole offer a few useful intuitions about how people might learn without having to experience such a death and transfiguration of mental life. Engage the person in a complex shared activity with another – there is a chemistry in the construction zone that allows one mind to appropriate another's thinking and that provokes new meanings. The mind the pupil finds in the construction zone may be that of the teacher; it may be embodied in designed learning environments set forth by microcomputers and media; it may come from expert adults, or from other children, brought with the child into the construction zone through computer networks.

The reach of the book is intriguing. On the one hand, it makes a solid contribution to a classic issue, how we might study mind in society. On the other, in a short but provocative section toward the end, it explores a new line of thought about the possible role of computers in education.

Sheldon H. White

Acknowledgments

The Oceanside School Project began in 1978 with initial funding from the National Institute of Education. The question we took on was how thinking can be identified and studied in varying social contexts. This is a practical problem for educational research because many people suspected that some children do better thinking in informal settings than in classroom or test settings. It is also a profound theoretical problem because it implies that the external social world is an integral part of cognitive processes and change.

As authors we each approached this question from quite different backgrounds, although we shared a commitment to understanding how the ordinary world of children was organized. Our thinking about these issues has taken place in a lively social environment in which a large number of members and friends of the Laboratory of Comparative Human Cognition contributed. For their help, advice and assistance we are grateful to Ann Brown, Bud Mehan, Byron Pepper, Cathy Echols, Christy Drale, David Middleton, David Markoff, Dianne Riley, Greg Griffin, Jan Hawkins, Jane Wellenkamp, Jean Lebeau, Jeff Gottfried, Jim Levin, Joe Campione, Jules Bagnairis, Julie Iodine, Karen Johnson, Karen Sheingold, Ken Traupmann, Laura Martin, Linda Hirsch, Margaret Riel, Marti tum Suden, Maryl Gearhart, Mitch Rabinowitz, Randy Souvinery, Robert Rowe, Ron Brown, Roy Pea, Shelley Goldman, Victor Flores, and Yaakov Kareev. The research would not have been possible without the cooperation of Principal Ray Kessler and teachers Kim Whooley, Will Nebblet and Marilyn Quinsaat and, of course, their students.

The research was supported by grant no. NIE-G-78-0159 from the National Institute of Education and by a grant from the Carnegie Corporation.

1 Introduction

A group of fourth graders are sitting around a table working with their teacher on division problems. The teacher puts a problem on the board and the children work out each step as the teacher writes out the developing solution. Turns are taken by the children; murmurs and eagerly raised hands signal group participation. The teacher asks questions, probes here and there, and fills in a little bit, managing to get each of the practice problems on the board. Something new is being constructed which we can see in the way the children begin to respond and in the way that the teacher works with their answers as the lesson progresses. Cognitive change – change in thinking and knowing – is clearly taking place as part of the instructional interaction. But where is the "cognition"? How do the children's cognitive processes change as they interact with the teacher and other students? These are the questions we address.

We take up the thesis that cognitive change is as much a social as an individual process. We examine the social interactions in which cognitive change is constructed so as to begin putting together a theory that shows how the individual and social worlds are entirely intertwined. We argue that to avoid dead ends in cognitive theory and educational practice, we have to go beyond citing individual factors and social factors as separable influences on cognitive change. At the same time, we attempt to break down the barriers between theory and practice by finding ways to use, as our laboratories, classrooms and other real settings which are the construction zones for cognition.

Our central point, that cognitive change must be regarded as both a social and an individual process, leads us to undertake the four main tasks of our classroom research. First, we study students who are low performers in school. These students are important to our work both because of the serious practical problems involved for educators and

1

because differences in performance often relate to differences in how children interpret school tasks. The differences and problems provide the additional windows on cognition and cognitive processes that we need for analysis. Second, we examine the differences between research and educational practice. We find repeatedly that the two endeavors run into conflict because of opposing goals and methods; we also find that the interaction of the two can yield important insights about the process of cognitive change. Third, we study methods for analyzing cognitive change as it occurs in a variety of settings not restricted to the traditional laboratory tasks. Neither ordinary laboratory measures nor traditional interactive coding schemes capture the flow between social and individual processes. Our focus on the intertwining of the two raises critical issues concerning what the object of study, or unit of analysis, should be. Finally, we continue to construct a theory of the process of cognitive change. When people with different goals, roles, and resources interact, the differences in interpretation provide occasions for the construction of new knowledge. The changes take place in socially mediated interactions that we, following Vygotsky (1978, 1986, 1987), call the "Zone of Proximal Development." Our theory is concerned with the outcomes and direction of change. Cognitive change does not happen in a closed, determined system. Productive change is possible, as is change for the worse, depending on the constructive processes in the zone.

Our goal is to illustrate the importance of including the social world in a theory of cognitive change, especially a theory that hopes to have practical implications for improved education. We frame our inquiries both in terms of current theorizing in cognitive science and other background considerations in developmental psychology, discourse analysis and cross-situational comparisons. In subsequent chapters we outline our methodological approach to classroom research and our theoretical approach to cognitive change. In four of the chapters, we take up specific cases of classroom activities on which we build the case that cognitive change is a process of interactive construction.

Cognitive change and cognitive science

We address several audiences who share an interest in the processes by which human beings acquire and use knowledge. One focus is the group of scholars who have come to be identified as cognitive scientists (Gardner, 1985; Norman, 1980). Of equal importance is the community of practitioners and teacher educators who look to cognitive theory for guidance in improving education. (See, for instance, the journals *Theory into Practice* and *Cognition and Instruction*.) Each group is reflected in our attempt to reinterpret cognitive science on the basis of the confrontation with classroom realities in the project we describe here. While we cannot pretend to have solved the problems that educational practitioners face daily, we can provide a perspective on current cognitive science which will help to delineate its strengths and weaknesses as a source of recommendations on how to redesign education. We hope also that our arguments concerning current methods and theories in cognitive research will help to persuade cognitive scientists to expand their domain to include the social processes which we believe are critical to explaining cognitive change.

At the heart of cognitive science, as thus far conceived, is the idea that it is possible to construct explicit, implementable models of complex psychological processes (Norman, 1980; Simon, 1980). This focus of attention follows from the scientific interest, articulated by Herbert Simon, in "physical symbol systems" such as the computer or the human brain. We agree with Simon's characterization of the mind as an artifact rather than as a "natural" system. This position is consistent with the sociohistorical theory (Vygotsky, 1978; Luria, 1978; Leont'ev, 1981) that we draw upon in our analysis of cognitive change. Where we differ from many of our colleagues in cognitive science is in our primary interest in man-made *systems of social activity*. A game of poker, work in a factory, a classroom lesson and a psychological experiment are all artificial systems in Simon's sense. But they are systems organized *among* as well as *within* human beings. *The physical symbol systems that constitute cognition are materially present in the organization of people – in their interactions – as well as in their brains.* Like Simon and other cognitive scientists, we set out to "model" a complex psychological process. But we did not seek to embody our model in a computer program. Rather we set out to create, in an elementary-school classroom, a series of theoretically motivated curriculum units in which we could observe the interactive process of teaching and learning.

While it might be conceded that cognitive science can logically be extended to systems of social interaction, the fact that such extensions have not played much of a part in contemporary cognitive science naturally raises a question: why bother? Artificial cognitive systems are complex enough in machine form, where we have a great deal of control over the elements that enter into the system, rendering it *closed* for analytic purposes. When we start to consider live people engaging in social interaction we have to contend with an *open* system (Bartlett, 1932; Norman, 1983). The participants' perspectives on the activity never coincide completely, and several interpretations of an individual's behavior may be simultaneously active (Bruce & Newman, 1978). While cognitive scientists have begun to approach more open systems in their analyses of ill-structured tasks (Greeno, 1978), the problem of including social interaction in the arena of cognitive science may be too tough a nut to crack (Simon, 1976).

Perhaps, though, the challenge of studying cognitive change in an open system can be productive. Just as the constraints and discipline of developing a computer-implementable model have deeply affected the vocabulary, procedures and theories of cognitive scientists, so might the challenge of developing models that conform to what we find to be the properties of man-made social activity.

In the "sciences of the artificial," as Simon (1981) argues, descriptions of how a system works are never far removed from questions about how to make it work better. Like those in other branches of cognitive science, we are interested in creating a better system and our work is intended to be of special relevance to social scientists and educators who are responsible for designing educational environments. Instruction has also been an important topic in cognitive science (Resnick, 1987a; Klahr, 1976; Glaser, 1978–87; Tuma & Rief, 1980; Sleeman & Brown, 1982). But the primary methods in cognitive science, focused as they are on modeling individual processes, are unable to bring the perspective of the social organization of instruction into the cognitive scientists' theoretical and practical activities.

Our central contribution is to focus on the instructional interaction as the locus of the constructive activity which constitutes cognitive change. This brings us face to face with the practice of teaching. By focusing directly on intellectual problems currently of concern to cognitive scientists and that seem to coincide with difficulties in educational practice, we can maximize the utility of our work. As the discussion proceeds, we hope to establish that it is not only possible, but very useful, to carry out extensions of cognitive science to include social interaction in educational settings. In this effort we make contact with recent advances within cognitive science which have resulted from examination of formal and informal learning settings (Collins, Brown & Newman, in press; Lave, 1988; Resnick 1987b). We want to argue further that for the crucial issue of cognitive *change*, inclusion of the social environment is a *necessity*.

To begin with, however, we want to summarize the steps and the practical concerns that led us to this formulation. Our current work represents a synthesis of research traditions which have up to now mostly gone their separate ways. To help motivate the discussions which follow, we will present the initial problems that were posed to us in narrative form, briefly tracing the history that led up to our attempts to combine cognitive and social analyses. Telling a story is a way to emphasize that we are responding to practical, historical problems as well as purely abstract scientific ones and to emphasize that the synthesis we are attempting is still being worked out.

Initial problems

The approach to the problem of cognitive change discussed in this book resulted from the convergence of three research programs. The problems we outline in this section emerged in relation to debates about cultural deprivation and context specificity. In the 1970's, a profound problem in the analysis of language use and cognitive processes had been posed by William Labov (1972). Labov reported a case in which an eight-year-old black child was being interviewed by a large, friendly white interviewer, in order to establish his language competence. The interviewer put objects on the table and posed problems like, "Tell me everything you can about this." The child answered with single words or short phrases separated by pauses up to 20 seconds. On another occasion with a black interviewer who changed the topic to street fighting, the child still gave short minimal answers. It was not until the interviewer brought along a supply of potato chips, included the child's best friend, sat down on the floor and introduced taboo topics that the kinds of responses

changed. Now the two children not only went beyond one-word answers but began actively competing for the floor.

Investigations of the language elicited in non-school settings reveal
that there is nothing second rate about the language systems that the
children used. Different from the language used in school and used
for writing, yes; worse, no. So, if the children have developed their
linguistic competence and their language is not inferior to the language used in schools or tests, why should there be a problem about
educating the children? And an education problem there clearly was,
and still is, for children like the eight-year-old black child in Labov's
example. How is it that once the child enters school a language difference comes to be a "deficit" for the child's cognitive growth?

Problem 1: Cultural mismatch or school structuring?

In general, work relating language difference to inequality
of educational outcome has taken two paths: the cultural match–
mismatch hypothesis and the structuring school hypothesis. First,
there is some support for the hypothesis that mismatch between the
language systems freely used by the children and the one used for
school discourse could be a locus of the educational problem. For
example, Hall, Cole, Reder & Dowley (1977) demonstrated that in
the free recall of narrative text, speakers whose home language is
Black Vernacular English were better at recalling texts in Black English than texts in Standard School English; while the opposite results
were obtained for speakers whose home language matched that of
Standard School English. However, even within that study, there was
reason to doubt that the match–mismatch hypothesis could account
fully for school failure: Hall et al. also found that the difference disappeared during probed recall. The advantage of a "match" between
the language system freely used and the one called for in a particular
setting can be overcome quite easily depending on the nature of the
task.

More reason for doubt about the adequacy of a mismatch explanation for educational problems came from the work of sociolin-
guists. Syntactic and phonological differences among dialects could
be clearly identified, and correlations could be established between
speaking a non-mainstream variety of English and having limited suc-

cess in school, particularly with respect to literacy. However, analyses of the language demands in reading and writing tasks failed to reveal the basis for the mainstream language advantage. A clear analysis developed about standardized test failure – many norm-referenced tests that purported to test reading development or syntactic proficiency were shown to need a "truth in packaging" component indicating that the test was really about whether the child could do reading and grammar in Standard English, not just do reading or grammar. Moratoriums on testing because of language and culture bias were sought and sometimes provided. However, the nagging reality of children failing to learn in addition to failing tests remained. One solid finding of this early sociolinguistic work on the problem of school failure was related to language attitudes – given tape-recorded samples of speech, subjects provide a wide range of negative judgments about the intelligence, employability, and general worth of those samples that can be considered non-mainstream varieties. In the days of Pygmalion in the Classroom (Rosenthal & Rubin, 1980) and the heightened awareness of the power of teachers' expectations, the language attitude findings could be interpreted in relation to the second hypothesis about inequality in education – the structuring of school failure.

In this context, the Center for Applied Linguistics undertook a large-scale study of the relation between the functions of language and early schooling tasks. Learning from the earlier sociolinguistic investigations that revealed the existence of variations but then revealed the irrelevance of such variety to school tasks, this study began with an investigation of classroom talk encountered in early education in terms of its uses and pragmatic design, where any mismatch should be most apparent. Working with a very successful private primary school, they found some aspects of the pragmatic features of talk to be varying among children, some of it according to age, some according to aspects of the social situation. But they found no correlation between this language variation and different degrees of success among the children. Variation among the children in their language use even failed to correlate with the teachers' perception of the children as more or less successful. They found no empirical or rational analysis that supported a one-to-one relation between certain (or a certain set of) language functions and academic success. Thus, even if further work revealed differences between the classroom talk of users of non-mainstream varieties of English and standard school English, a mismatch hypothesis could not really provide a full account for school failure.

At this point, the study of functional language brought the CAL group into full contact with the structuring failure hypothesis. Mehan in San Diego, Cazden, Erickson, and Shultz in Massachusetts, and McDermott and Cole in New York had been looking at schools very different from the one in which the CAL team had worked; while the CAL group was looking at a successful school and privileged children, these other investigators were face to face with the pheno- menon of failure. The work could be linked to the earlier sociolin- guistic language attitude findings: Perhaps there was not a mysterious Pygmalion that translated low expectations about children who spoke a non-mainstream and undervalued variety of English into school failure; perhaps both the attitudes and the failure were me- diated by particular structures encountered in schools (structures of lessons, structures of discourse) which failed to promote learning for children whose differences from the teacher and the mainstream could be easily noticed in their language. It was clear that the talk exchanged in lessons differed from the talk exchanged elsewhere in life (Mehan, 1979; Sinclair & Coulthard, 1975); this difference would be a mismatch but, more, the unusual talk found in schools could be the peculiarity which produced the failure that was seen. In that case, one would expect *not* to see the peculiarities in the success- ful school for privileged children where, apparently, failure was *not* being structured. But all the structures found in the "failure" studies were present in the successful school, Griffin and her colleagues found out (Griffin & Humphrey, 1978).[1]

Problem 2: Comparing performance across contexts

Since neither specific structures of language/dialect nor structures of language use/pragmatics covaried with success and

---

[1] More recent work by Heath (1982) and Cook-Gumperz & Gumperz (1981) that includes positive acts of intervention shows how schooling can be restructured to accommodate widely varying patterns of child socialization, providing a productive blending of the "mismatch" hypothesis and the structuring hypothesis.

failure, more needed to be known about the *processes* of performance in school, if progress was to be made on the problems of school failures. Perhaps a more advanced combination hypothesis would work: what children had learned to do and say in order to learn at home could match or mismatch what they needed to do to learn in school as presently structured. Such a hypothesis rested on the untested assumption that it is possible to make valid comparisons from language use and cognitive activity in the home to their analogous forms in school. All such lines of reasoning imply that inferences about psychological processes in one setting (the home, the school, the street corner conversation, etc.) can be validly applied to analysis of a second setting. But it was not clear that there existed any methodology strong enough to warrant such claims.

As a first step toward tackling this dilemma, Cole and his colleagues at the Rockefeller University (Lois Hood, Ray McDermott, and Ken Traupmann) undertook a direct investigation of whether cognitive tasks could be identified and studied in a non-school setting (Cole, Hood & McDermott, 1978). They videotaped a single classroom of 18 children. They created some new settings in addition to those encountered in the school, each offering variations to permit them to see how cognitive tasks are influenced by their immediate social context. At one extreme they created a battery of tests that sampled categories of cognitive activities believed to be central to psychological functions in the everyday world as well as the school: remembering, classifying, problem solving and so on. At the other extreme they created after-school clubs where the children came to cook, play board games and engage in a variety of science projects. In between was the classroom: formal lessons, study time, adult-directed discussion. This range may not be a very great swatch of reality, tied closely as it is to school at both ends. But it was greater than any researcher had been able to record on videotape before.

When they went to the classroom to discover the kinds of cognitive tasks that made up their test battery they could find them and a lot more like them. Although they were dealing with a relatively "open" classroom, there were many times each day when children could be seen classifying, remembering and problem solving. The researchers even began to work up a coding scheme whereby they could track the source of the cognitive task (the teacher, a book, another child, self-initiated) and the child's response to it.

This happy enterprise was interrupted by the start of the club sessions. Initially the researchers were occupied with the raw mechanics of getting the children to the club site and keeping them happy. Then they began to look for cognitive tasks during the club sessions. They saw a great deal of activity – the noise level in the club room was enough to convince all of their colleagues that someone was hard at work. But except on rare occasions it was very difficult to identify any of the cognitive tasks that they had posed for children in their testing sessions or seen during observations in the classroom. Somehow cakes were getting baked, plants grown, rat mazes constructed and electric circuits lit, without anyone doing anything that a cognitive psychologist could recognize as thinking; they found it difficult to discover cognitive task-like problems and virtually impossible to specify in traditional task-analytic terms how children responded on those rare occasions when they thought that such a problem had in fact occurred.

In the ensuing year they intensively studied the videotapes they had collected in order to discover the characteristics of the ways in which behavior was organized in each of the various settings. Even cursory analysis showed that they could not attribute the differences among the settings simply to the existence or nonexistence of academic content. To bake a cake one needs to read recipes, measure, and keep track of what one has done. To get through a test one has to engage in coordinated social interaction with another person. All situations they studied were a mixture of "cognitive" and "social" activities. To be sure, the density of each, or perhaps the salience of each to the casual observer, was different. In the tests or in those parts of the school day where children were seen to be engaged in cognitive tasks, social interaction seemed like a part of the background. In the clubs, social interaction was *rarely* in the background.

When the researchers began to make comparisons of the children in the two settings, they had the strong impression that the children who were the class "stars" in school did not shine especially as a group during the club sessions. Nor were the class dunces readily identifiable. A little reflection will suggest that this observation poses an embarrassing paradox. Having just said that cognitive tasks could not be identified in the clubs, the researchers turned around and claimed that they simultaneously discovered children who seemed to be cognitively more competent in the club than in school.

Once they made the judgment that some children behaved more competently when facing the task of baking cake in the club than doing a reading or measuring task in school, Cole and his colleagues and made contact with the initial question for the present work:

> What does it mean, in terms of the methodology upon which assessment of cognitive processes is based, to say that you have *the same task in different settings?* And if you don't know how to identify "same tasks," what is the basis for your judgement that some children perform well in one version of "the" task and not another?

It was clear at this point that an answer to the question was going to require a cognitive theory that could handle non-test situations. If our studies were to be relevant to the practical problems of education, we could not afford to misrepresent children who did not get along well under test conditions. It was also becoming increasingly clear that understanding how children learned new things was critical to understanding how the process might be going wrong. An approach was needed that would integrate the cognitive and social aspects of children in classrooms. We had to be able to handle not only a wide variety of social situations but also how children learned to operate successfully within them.

Problem 3: Indeterminacy as a key to change

The key concept that refocused our work from questions of differences between settings and children at a single time to questions about changes over time was the indeterminacy of speech. Drawing on Vygotsky's (1986) *Thought and Language,* and Bakhtin's (Volosinov, 1973) work on indirect discourse, Griffin was led to pay attention to the indeterminacy of collaborative utterances in the construction of lessons (Griffin & Humphrey, 1978). Teacher utterances, for example, often served multiple functions: a question to one child can also serve as an implicit negative evaluation of another child's answer. Not being able to give a single meaning to an utterance may appear to be an impossible problem for linguistic analysis. But the indeterminacy also leaves room for movement and change. The same issue arose in another set of studies of school discourse by one of the authors.

Newman, working with John Dore and Maryl Gearhart, attempted to describe the functions of nursery-school children's language in terms of "illocutionary force" or speech acts. These functional categories include such things as Questions, Requests for Permission, Promises and Assertions. As a first step toward functional analyses of language in a variety of settings, a coding system was devised by which utterances were assigned to speech act categories (Dore, Gearhart & Newman, 1978). This was not at all a straightforward task since (1) the function of utterances cannot be determined without considering the social context in which the utterance functions and (2) one finds that the children's and teacher's utterances were often the means for *creating* the social context. For example, it often appeared that when ownership was not already firmly established, a child's request for permission to play with a toy functioned to cede ownership to the other child (Newman, 1978). Coding speech acts was complex also because the teacher and children clearly had very different understandings of what the interaction was about – there was no single "correct" interpretation. Furthermore, these were not problems that could be solved by better coding methods or clearer category definitions. Language use, by its very nature, occurs within a realm of constantly constructed interpretations (McDermott & Tylbor, 1983; Newman & Bruce, 1986).

Gearhart & Newman (1980) conducted one study of cognitive change building on the systematic vagueness of nursery school discourse, providing a critical insight that is elaborated in our current work. They noticed that teachers very often made an interpretation of a child's action in terms of her own frame of reference. For example, at the art table the teacher almost always had a brief discussion with the children whenever they finished a drawing or painting. As structured by the teacher, these discussions often presupposed that the child had planfully created a picture of some object. The teacher asked questions like "What is this?" which the child could answer regardless of the process leading up to the "finished product." The process of drawing or painting in most cases was distinctly *not* directed toward creating a picture of something. Children often imitated each other, experimented with various markers and crayons and usually stopped because some other activity caught their interest, not because the drawing was "finished." The teacher–child discussions were interesting because they provided an interpretation of what the activity of drawing was supposed to be about from the teacher's point of view. By asking "What is this?" the teacher presupposes the markings on the paper represent or communicate something in particular, and her question indicates her retrospective interpretation. It appears that this process in which a teacher *appropriates* something a child does, interpreting it in terms of her own frame of reference, is a means by which cognitive change can take place. In the current research, this feature of social interaction is studied.

Such an interactive process of change depends on the very aspects of discourse that make it difficult to apply a static coding system: *the fact that there are two different interpretations of the context and the fact that the utterances themselves serve to change the interpretations.* Putting the issue this way makes apparent the connection to concerns about comparisons across contexts and about comparisons among cultural groups that Griffin and Cole had been working on.

The current work began with an assumption that the social and cognitive aspects of school and non-school activities could not be dealt with separately. Our initial strategy was to attempt to compare the same cognitive task in different social settings over time. This would require going well beyond naturalistic observations. As we detail in Chapter 2, we had to devise ways to create settings that would give us the control we needed to make inferences regarding cognition outside of the laboratory. Once we created such settings we could begin the analyses which are the topic of this book.

The plan for this book

Each of the seven chapters elaborates on the central idea that cognitive change is as much a social as an individual process. This simple idea has wide-ranging implications, which we trace. The synthesis of social and individual processes that we undertake is not something that fits easily into the traditional ways of speaking in cognitive science. Our exposition starts with some concrete details of how we worked in the classroom and of one example that illustrates some of the critical concepts. We then outline the theoretical concerns before presenting three more cases which expand on implications of the theory.

While we report on studies with two elementary-school classrooms, the contexts in which the teachers and children appear range from laboratory tasks to after-school clubs. Our analyses concern cognitive changes that happen over a matter of minutes to those that take months and even years. The four tasks that we set for ourselves at the beginning of this chapter recur in these contexts and levels of analysis. First, each of the chapters, but chapters 6 and 7 in particular, are concerned with students who are low performers in school. Second, the differences between research and educational practice were evident throughout our activities in the classrooms and are specifically reported in Chapters 2, 5 and 8. Third, new methods for studying cognitive change are illustrated in Chapters 2, 3, 5, 6 and 7. Fourth, the application of a theoretical position which is specifically outlined in Chapter 4 is demonstrated in all the chapters.

In the second chapter, "Building Tasks into Curriculum Units," we explain the specific strategy used in our project for making the same task happen in different settings. We designed a set of special curriculum units for third- and fourth-grade classrooms which allowed us to instantiate tasks in a variety of classroom and nonclassroom organizations and thereby obtain sufficient control to pull apart some of the tight intertwining of individual and social processes.

The third chapter, "Making Goals Happen," reports one outcome of our cross-setting research strategy. An analysis of a task in two different settings shows how laboratory tasks systematically obscure the process by which the subject comes to have the goal of the task. The goal is already prepared by the researcher as a condition for obtaining sufficient control over the experimental situation. The fact that a subject, especially a child subject, may have an alternative analysis of the task is either corrected during the instruction phase or is made invisible by procedures and the coding scheme used to measure the subject's performance. By comparing laboratory and peer activity versions of the "same task," we can clearly see this limitation on the laboratory setting. But we can also see that both the researcher and the teacher must *appropriate* the child's actions to give them meaning in terms of a new system of activity.

After concretely illustrating a number of fundamental concepts in Chapter 3, we then set out the essentials of our theoretical approach. Chapter 4, "Basic Concepts for Discussing Cognitive Change," articulates the essentials of our theoretical approach. We borrow heavily from Vygotsky's sociohistorical theory, treating social interaction and culture in a principled way as sources of change. We focus on several interrelated aspects of the theory which we believe form a sound basis for an educationally useful theory of cognitive change. An important idea is that skills are practiced and understandings achieved in inter- action with others before children can do them on their own. This is the basis for Vygotsky's famous concept, the "*zone of proximal devel- opment.*" The theory presupposes that there are always multiple points of view (analyses) on any object, and it is by virtue of the interaction of these differing analyses that change is possible. In in- structional interaction, the teacher's analysis "appropriates" (takes up and makes use of) the child's actions into a wider system. Obvi- ously, such a theory contrasts sharply with other positions, particu- larly concerning the continuity and direction of cognitive change. Since new cognitive structures have their origin in social interaction, change often produces discontinuities with the child's earlier under- standings. But also as a consequence of their origin in social inter- action, not all change is for the better. In many cases, the interactions can have detrimental effects or result in changes that cannot be as- sessed as better or worse.

The basic concepts are applied and extended in the following three chapters. In the fifth chapter, "Assessment versus Teaching," we discuss how Vygotsky's concept of the zone of proximal development provides a method for assessing children while in interaction with adults. The method uses the social events as a way of tracking cogni- tive change which contrasts with ordinary testing methods which try to minimize the impact of the social context. Our attempts to use this assessment method reveal crucial limitations that arise when the ob- server's task is teaching rather than research. From the researcher's point of view there is an area of indeterminacy because the teacher necessarily takes every opportunity to teach rather than waiting for children to fail at the task. In traditional analysis of the teaching/ learning process, this indeterminacy is an impediment to clear-cut analysis. From the current perspective, however, open-ended social interaction allows the researcher to study the multiple paths and endpoints for cognitive change.

The sixth chapter, "Social Mediation Goes into Cognitive Change,"

illustrates the social construction of knowledge in the Zone of Proximal Development. The analysis in this case is based on data from a
set of division lessons which the students enter with markedly different levels of prior knowledge and skill. We find that the crucial step
in the division algorithm was neither taught directly nor invented
spontaneously by the children. Rather, it emerged in the interaction
as the teacher appropriated the trial and error attempts of the children and used them to instantiate the expert strategy. Differences in
ability groups led to differences in this interactive process such that
the lower ability groups were unable to move beyond the teacher's
explicit instructions.

The seventh chapter, "How the West Has Won," examines a set
of lessons in which ability group differences disappeared and then
reappeared. This analysis makes clear that while different understandings of lesson content may at first coexist, one understanding is
systematically given preference. The mental-cultural tools involved
in these lessons provide grounds for a reexamination of hypotheses
about schooling inequity. The chapter demonstrates the cultural mediation of cognitive change through an analysis of discourse found in
classrooms such as the ones we have examined.

We conclude by specifying the implications of our work for
researchers in the cognitive sciences and for educators and others
concerned with improving the quality of education. A redefinition of
task in terms of its source, social constraints, and multiple perspectives provides the starting point for another look at appropriation and
multidirectional change, We reexamine also the role of the teacher,
contrasting the teacher's task with that of the researcher. The differences between these roles, while often leading to conflict, are also
the key to classroom research that examines the full range of contexts
and processes of cognitive change. Our conclusions for instructional
design, including the use of new technologies, follows from our
analysis of cognitive change as a social as much as an individual
process.

2 Building tasks into curriculum units

It is one thing to arrive at an abstract specification of the way that learning and development occur in instructional settings and quite another to embody those ideas in a set of scientific activities that can provide empirical support, and hopefully a basis for improving later educational practice. In this chapter we explain the research strategy we evolved, including some of the false steps that eventually led us to a productive methodology.

Each of these steps was in fact a formative experiment in which we took a cognitive task and planted it in classroom and club settings. It was not always easy to get the task to take root. Teachers and children constitute a complex ecology, calling for intense collaboration in which both teachers and researchers must attempt to make sense of the others' goals and methods. The demands of a cognitive experiment involving cross-situational comparisons must find a way to meet the educational imperatives of the classroom (Quinsaat, 1980). Making the same task happen in more than one classroom context required a new approach that goes beyond observation of naturally occurring events while not obscuring the ordinary settings that are the object of study.

Making the "same task" happen in different settings

When Cole and his colleagues started their earlier project, they thought they had built the possibility of cross-situational comparison into the structure of the activities that occurred in the three basic settings (test, school, club). The tests had initially been designed to sample school-like tasks, so one could be confident that the tasks would appear in the classroom (as they did). The researchers chose

17

a variety of cooking and nature activities specifically because these activities involve reading, measurement, remembering and other cognitive skills that are the focus of the school. In fact, the reasonableness of that idea was used to convince teachers and parents that the clubs would be a good "educational experience" for the children. Yet when they came to look for tasks in the club activities, something about the social organization rendered it difficult to identify cognitive tasks in a form that they could acknowledge as cognitive scientists.

Crudely speaking, the source of the difficulty in making cross-situational cognitive comparisons is that different social constraints operate on people in different contexts, be they in school or out. The psychologist's task (classifying, paired associated learning, logical reasoning) is not a physical object in the world, although it often includes physical objects. A task is, rather, a set of actions, the goal of which is prespecified by the psychologist along with a set of constraints that must be honored in meeting that goal.

A second problem concerned the specification of goals. When we stated in the previous paragraph that the psychologist sets the goal for the subject as part of the defining characteristics of a cognitive task, we were adopting the professional shorthand. In fact, even casual analysis of a single testing situation quickly reveals that an enormous amount of "social work" goes into maintaining the psychologist's task as a focus of attention (Mehan, 1979). Subjects often are as anxious to demonstrate their friendliness or intelligence, or simply to get-it-over-as-quickly-as-possible, as they are to "think hard" (Cicourel et al., 1970). Test situations are designed to minimize the impact of these alternative goals. Large groups of subjects are usually run on quantifiable tasks so that reliable and "valid" conclusions regarding thinking can be achieved.

We don't wish to question the utility of this approach here. (But see Cole, Hood & McDermott, 1978.) What is crucial to point out for the current work is that in non-test settings (including the school classroom and clubs), the multiple goals that occupy each individual at any single moment are very difficult to ignore because the settings are rarely so constrained that they prevent people from working to achieve several goals at the same time. That means that we have to deal with some difficult problems of "task analysis" in order to think coherently about task similarity across contexts. Only very general characteristics of a restricted set of task environments can be specified ahead of time in a manner analogous to the way psychologists specify their cognitive tasks.

These earlier attempts to specify how cognitive tasks and behaviors vary across social contexts convinced us that the solution would not come about through the systematic application of any established techniques of discourse or cognitive analysis. (We report on our investigation of such data analyses using data from this project in Griffin, Cole & Newman, 1982). Identifying cognitive tasks outside of the laboratory would require a novel synthesis of methods.

Having concluded on the basis of the previous work that statements about children "doing the same task" better or worse in one of the settings are difficult (if not impossible) to warrant if we depend on discovering "naturally" occurring tasks, we decided in the project we report here to make as certain as we could that the same task occurred and recurred in a variety of settings. At the outset we knew that there would be limits to the degree of "sameness" that we could arrange. But we did not know on the basis of our earlier failures what those limits might be. We phrased our strategy as follows: *Let's try to make a cognitive task happen several times and see how different social settings pull it apart in different ways.*

We worked closely with teachers and club leaders to construct a set of activities (one-to-one tutorials, small group lessons, child-guided work groups), all of which had a specific problem structure embedded within them. So instead of waiting around for a recognizable cognitive task to appear, we deliberately set out to find ways to make hypothetical "same tasks" happen in several settings inhabited by the same children. We put the term "same task" in quotes because the sense in which two tasks can ever be considered the same is a central question for this analysis; we want to explore it, not beg it. It must be said at the outset that we had no illusions that a cognitive task could be specified independent of its social context. Our orientation was quite the opposite.

Social construction of cognitive tasks

In earlier work we described the necessary attributes of a cognitive task:

To be well defined, a task ought to yield at least information about the goal of the activity, the initial conditions confronting the informant, and the set of elements in the task environment that the informant confronts at any time. In other words, a well-defined task specifies all of the possible stimuli which the subject might have to attend to in the course of proceeding from one point in the solution of a task to another.

Next the cognitive psychologist requires a circumscribed and predetermined set of behaviors that are allowable within the task environment. If behaviors that are *not* a part of the analytic system have to be taken into account, it is not possible to specify the probability of one event (a response) relating to other events (stimuli) because the sample spaces for both sides of the function are of indeterminate size.

Finally, one must have a model which specifies the relationship between various states of the task environment (the stimuli) and the various "moves" (the behavior) of the informant within the task environment. "Cognitive process" then refers only to the model-generated function relating behaviors in the task environment to its different states. (LCHC, 1978, pp. 53–4)

As this description implies, a cognitive task is always a social construction with two aspects. The first aspect arises from the broad historical context of the psychologist's work. The second arises from the immediate "on-line" interaction between the experimenter and subject. Scientists who construct models and design task environments are a part of, and act in response to, the setting provided by the sociohistorical conditions of their discipline (Cicourel, 1974; Frake, 1977; Wiser & Carey, 1983). Cognitive processes and the tasks that allow them to appear in psychological theories are constrained by the apparatus, the theoretical constructs, the analytical procedures, and the successes and failures that the psychologists' community make available as the defining practices of the discipline.

The social construction of cognitive tasks, in the second sense, results from the psychologist's role as a silent partner in the subject's behavior. In the quotation above, the authors relied on a figure of speech (metonymy) which obscures the actor. It is not really the "task" that "yield[s]...information...about goals...conditions... elements" or that "specifies" anything; it is the experimenter who, as it is said, "runs" the subject and the task. Similarly, the experimenter is the agent behind the expressions "are allowable" and "to be taken into account." In the microcosmic society of an experiment, the experimenter has a lot of control "on-line," being responsible for what the subject is supposed to do, when, and, to a large measure, how. But the construction does not totally reside in the instructions issued to the subject and on-line adjustments; it is also there in the subsequent analysis. Presented a string of digits to remember (743289), the subject might, for instance, say, "4, 7, 2, 8" under certain conditions. The psychologist can then conclude, for example, that the subject did not say 3, the subject did not say the last digit, the subject got two digits out of order, the subject is below average at the task, the subject is giving evidence of a memory deficit. It is hard to imagine such conclusions unless one knows about digit-span tests, experiments, and the performance of large and varied populations of subjects. These sorts of attributions could not be made without the co-construction of the utterance "4, 7, 2, 8" by the subject and by the psychologist as analyst.

In this project, in order to examine the social construction of psychological tasks, we had to change both aspects of the usual constructive activities of the experimenter. In addition to broadening the choice of settings that the discipline has given prominence for study, we wanted some of the settings to allow for more on-line and interpretive control by the subjects. Another perspective on our efforts to do this can be gained by considering research which uses the "problem isomorph" notion.

Our use of "problem isomorphs"

When we set out to make "same tasks" happen, our idea was to create a set of what are called "problem isomorphs" in cognitive psychology. Problem isomorphs are a set of problems which share an abstract structure but differ in concrete content (e.g., Reed, Ernst & Banerji, 1974; Gick & Holyoak, 1980). So in a classic example from the problem isomorph literature, subjects must transport missionaries and cannibals from one side of a river to another under severe constraints (e.g., the cannibals must never outnumber the missionaries; the boat used for transportation can hold only two characters). Transfer is then studied using hobbits and orcs or husbands and wives as characters in problems, isomorphic to the first. In each case the goal is prespecified and the logical analyses identical. The researcher does a lot of work to arrange for the subject to know what the goal is ahead of time and to ensure that all of the conditions and the constraints that are important to the interpretation of the data are adhered to.

In cognitive psychological studies, problem isomorphs are used to study the effects on a subject's performance after experience with a problem of the same kind. Questions about the generality of a concept, or transfer of training, are often addressed with the isomorph apparatus. Every effort is made to change only the content of the problem, leaving the abstract form of the procedures, initial conditions, legal moves, and goal unchanged.

Puzzling results of recent work with problem isomorphs point to the problems we are raising here, couched in different terms. Sometimes, in spite of the clear legitimacy of the psychologist's claim that the two problems are the "same," and in spite of extensive control over the materials and the subject's behavior, the subject's response makes it look as if the tasks are different. From the analyst's point of view this is reported as a failure to generalize, as a failure to transfer training, or as asymmetrical transfer between presumed isomorphs. From our point of view, it can also be understood as a failure to make, to construct socially, the "same task" on two occasions.

Our research includes the examination of settings where "on-line" social control of the task that we hope to "run" is handed over to participants who are not constrained by the rules of psychology as a discipline. Even the issue of whether they will bother to undertake (or succeed in) the social construction of "our task" is a significant problem. In fact, transformations of the social organization of the tasks that we studied drastically changed the constraints on behavior, thereby rendering the tasks instantly different according to widely shared ideas of what constitutes a task in cognitive psychology. It was our hope that by highlighting the way in which our efforts *failed* to make the "same task" occur in different settings, we could arrive at a clearer specification of the class of social constructions represented by such activities as tests and experiments. Giving away the usual scientist's control, we hoped, would let us see that we could not know enough to see if we retained full control.

The growth of the cycles

Our project was conducted in a school in the northern part of San Diego County. In the first year we worked in a third–fourth-grade combination, team-taught classroom. In the second year, we worked in the fourth-grade classroom of one of the original teachers and with some of the original children. Our data corpus involves 80 children and three teachers sampled over the two-year period. During our time in the classrooms we worked with the teachers to design curriculum modules, each of which was intended as a formative experiment in creating the same task across a variety of contexts. Our topics ranged from science (e.g., electricity, animals, household chemicals) to mathematics (division), to social studies (Native American Indians, mapping), to a unit on memory and study skills. Each experiment taught us something about how to do the next one. We called each of the experiments a "cycle" because in each one we tried to repeat similar kinds of classroom events – large-group lessons, small-group activities, tutorials – but in a new topic domain. Between cycles, we spent time analyzing the outcomes and planning for the next cycle.

Each of these research "cycles" were also very much part of the classroom. From the teachers' point of view, each cycle was a curriculum unit in a subject area appropriate for a third- or fourth-grade classroom. We worked very closely with, and put heavy demands on, the teachers in our project. Two teachers had chosen to work together in the double-sized classroom that they invited us to join; at the beginning of our planning, they chose a third teacher to join their team to help with the extra work our presence would entail. Not only did we plan all the cycles together, but after almost every videotaped lesson, we replayed the tape and asked the teacher participant to make comments on how the lesson went, what he or she noticed as unusual or surprising about any of the children, and so on. Then we often got into a long discussion of how the next day's lessons could or should be modified to take advantage of some opportunity or to avoid some pitfall that became clear in the viewing sessions. Our initial notion in conducting these sessions was the need to bring other perspectives to bear on our data in order to triangulate on the phenomena (Cicourel, 1974). As the project progressed, however, the striking differences between the teacher and researcher perspectives became a topic in itself.

In some respects the practitioners and researchers had the same relationship as others who had been involved in classroom research (Florio & Walsh, 1980; Mehan, 1979). Florio and Walsh labeled the teacher's role "Observant Participant," giving the impression that researchers and practitioners collaborated in finding and making observations about the classroom. However, while in previous classroom work researchers were primarily observers, in this project, researchers set up and participated in specific tasks in order to explore systematically the ways in which cognitive tasks are influenced by the interactional and curricular variations necessary to run a classroom. The problem of coordinating the needs of cognitive research with the ongoing business of teaching and learning in the classroom had to be confronted continually.

We completed seven cycles, three the first year and four the second. This section presents a brief history of our work together – the failures as well as the successes.

Five working principles constrained our choices of cycle topics throughout the project.

1. *The topic and lesson plans should be known ahead of time to both researchers and teachers.* We were not interested in capturing and analyzing only the teacher's ordinary classroom events as we might if this were an ethnography; nor were we interested in taking the children into a laboratory environment as we might if this were a traditional, experimental approach. We knew how hard it was to locate tasks *post hoc* as they appeared in ordinary events, and we knew that methods that rely only on laboratory environments are overly confining for our purposes. Our strategy dictated that we plan the content of the lessons jointly with the classroom teachers and observe the consequences of their implementation. We tried to be as explicit as possible, knowing that we could never be totally explicit.

2. *Each topic covered should be embedded in a variety of socially organized events.* A basic motivation for our work was to determine how different social organizations help or hinder performance for different children. Hence, we wanted teaching events of different types and some more casual events that were outside of the ordinary school rules of institutional relations. The results were five different configurations of participant structures:

   a. Teacher-led large-group lessons: These are lessons conducted by the teacher with a group composed of approximately 20 students; they seldom occurred in the classroom outside of our special curriculum units.

b. Teacher-led small-group lessons: These are organized such that five or six children work intensively with the teacher; slightly larger groups were common in the classroom without our intervention.
c. Child-only small-group lessons: Groups of children worked together on an assigned task (often workbooks or other written materials) without direct access to a teacher; these were familiar events in the classroom.
d. Tutorials: The teacher or a researcher works one-to-one with a child; these were rare outside of our research units, except for one-to-one sessions related to classroom management.
e. Clubs: A member of the research staff interacts with students, either in a community setting, or at the University, about the material covered in the cycles, but in a less didactic and more recreational format.

3. *Each topic should be one which is relatively novel, so that knowledge and experience from prior exposure, in school and out, would not be so likely to intrude and differentiate among the children in ways that we had no access to in our data records.* (Here, at least, we join forces with the impulse behind Ebbinghaus' much criticized nonsense syllable strategy for memory research.) For some of the units, we had task situations that could function as pretests (e.g., for the division cycle described in Chapter 6 and the chemicals cycle, Chapters 3 and 5); for most, we depended on the novel nature of the tasks to ward off the possibility of unknown differences among the children at the start of the unit.

4. *Each topic should be unobtrusive, existing as a topic that would normally be taught children of third- and fourth-grade age in that school district.* That is, our cycles had to be understandable as educationally important curriculum units. We adopted this principle for three reasons: (a) the teachers had a responsibility to use classroom time educating the children in a way that was coherent with what the school and parents expected; (b) we were interested in the relevance of our work for ordinary education; and (c) we knew from our prior work that the organization of ordinary classrooms had sufficient similarity to the organization of psychological experiments so that we could use the psychological literature as a guide and critical base.

5. *The topics should be ones that bring out the best in the teaching situation and still yield enough variability in child performance so that the research could succeed.*

Under ordinary circumstances, these teachers presented the children with innovative practices and with "extra" adults, e.g., teacher-interns. So it was possible for us to fit in. In general, the children came to take our presence for granted, along with our microphones and video cameras. We sat in on the classroom outside of the time of our seven data collection periods, sometimes pressed into service as helpers by children or teachers. The children knew that we had jobs that involved figuring out about children growing up. Even before we collaborated with them in planning cycles, the teachers knew a good deal about the process and function of our kind of research, because their preservice training had been in a program that emphasized the research carried out in classrooms by sociologists and psychologists. In part because the teachers had an important role in planning and implementing our research cycles, our "curriculum modules" could look (to a child, intern, parent or principal) much like some of the special sequences that this group of three teachers would "team up" to produce without our intervention.

Our first try at implementing the working principles

The first cycle we tried to implement, the electricity cycle, highlights the difficulty we had in maintaining our working principles. Our first attempts to create the possibility of cross-situational comparison illustrates the complexity of the principle that the cycle topic should be well known by the researcher and the teacher ahead of time. It was not enough just to have the same content. As it turns out, and as we describe in the next section, an additional mediating device, which we call the "tracer," was needed.

At the time that we developed the electricity cycle, we had great confidence in the power of a content domain to organize the classroom activity so it could serve both research and pedagogical purposes. The topic of electricity *did* unify the first cycle and we had narrowed the topic to batteries and circuits, but that wasn't sufficient to give us the evidence we had hoped for. We still had not gotten to the point that there were clearly discernible elements in enough of the social configurations so that we could think productively about problem isomorphs and the "same" task appearing or failing to appear. The lack of specificity that hindered our research use of the cycle also created problems for the teachers and the students.

All of the people on the planning team were liberally educated and had a working knowledge of electricity, in particular the structure and functioning of batteries and circuits. However, as recent work has shown (e.g., Clement, 1982; DiSessa, 1982; Larkin, McDermott, Simon & Simon, 1980), the working knowledge we have of physics topics and the metaphors that we use to talk about them do not fit well with the science that we learn in formal education. The way we talk about electricity is so confined to specific metaphors (Gentner & Gentner, 1983) that it often fails to accommodate a new, crucial bit of physical evidence in the world or a contradictory statement offered by a conversational partner. Such opportunities to question or clarify our understandings can just slip by.

This kind of slippage happened in our planning for the electricity cycle. For example, one of the planners worked within the scope of a water pipe metaphor and another worked in an information processing metaphor when talking about electron flow; consequently, the questions, objections and suggestions offered during planning discussions were often incoherent but were "passable" for making lesson plans and arranging for lesson materials to be bought and made.

This problem is unlikely to arise in an experiment on concept learning in a laboratory, even if similar topics were investigated. In laboratory cognitive experiments, the experimenter can know a lot less about the topic than a teacher has to know because so much of the responsibility for producing coherence belongs to the model task analysis which generated the protocol governing the experimenter's and the subject's talk and action. Instructions set the frame and the rest is up to the subject.

Although we planned ideal lessons, i.e., scripts, ahead of time and provided the materials to be used, and even tried out the procedures on one-third of the class as a pilot study, we could not predict when a child's comment or question or blank stare would occur, nor could we predict how the teacher's response could be designed to "save" the ideal lesson. During the planning the teachers could not give us good "But suppose..." objections, and while they were teaching, we were unable to understand the teachers' on-line decisions about what to highlight and what to sacrifice when the unexpected events happened. It appeared that the metaphorical richness of the electricity concepts meant that we, and the teachers, had insufficient *on-line* control of the task to get the "electricity lessons" to work as problem isomorphs.

In assessing our progress at the end of the electricity cycle it was clear that we had to be far more specific in designing future cycles. It was not sufficient to depend on a *content domain* such as electricity. When it comes to observing the specific events, too many unexpected divergences and digressions led the children, teachers, and researchers astray.

It is not that the lessons and activities in the cycle were entirely unrelated. We had classroom discussions in a variety of social configurations that referred to the structure and functioning of either circuits or batteries. The children appeared to have a grasp of some new vocabulary and topics for conversation and performance on tests; they managed to get homemade light bulb–battery arrangements affixed to a plywood cutout of a Christmas tree. But there were no segments from one lesson that we could say were or were not the "same task" as other segments. We could not locate commonalities across the settings in terms of goals being set, conditions being met toward achieving them, material resources, products, or sequences of talk or writing relevant to such goals. We were naive in assuming that the fact that the activities were all on the same topic would give us the necessary analytic handle. A much more specific device, which we came to call a "tracer," was necessary to narrow our planning and execution of future cycles.

The tracers in the cycles

We resolved to choose a narrower focus for our next attempt at a cycle and a topic that would not engage the difficulties of talking through our divergent metaphors as electricity had. We needed tasks that we could be more clear about in our planning. It was also apparent that we needed some mediating device between the tasks and the "scripts" for the series of sessions of a cycle.

We borrowed the notion "tracer" from health care studies: A tracer is expected to appear if and only if some specific circumstances of interest are present; tracers may be objects or arrangements holding between objects. For example, an ear disease diagnosable in early adolescence can be a tracer for inadequate treatment of earaches that accompanied colds in earlier childhood. So we looked for tasks that could meet yet another condition: each cycle and each lesson in a cycle should have a task that has tracers that could appear no matter what the social configuration. *The tracers took the form of some bit of knowledge, procedure, set of actions or talk, or written symbol.* They were central to the problem structure that was "scripted" to occur in each of the sessions in a cycle. The tracer was designed to be useful if children recognized that they had been confronted with the "same task" in the new setting. Otherwise, we could notice its absence; a tracer embodied only in the "script" or associated only with the adult in a setting would be a good indicator that the task had disappeared! This set of constraints greatly increased the probability of finding good candidates for cognitive analysis and of uncovering how the "same task," under the different organizational conditions, is transformed, made easier or more difficult, or avoided entirely as far as the children are concerned.

Table 2.1 outlines the cycles and tracers reported throughout this book. In the first year, we did two additional cycles which profited from our experiences and from our use of tracers. In Chapter 7, our second cycle (on Native American social studies) is described in more detail. The tracers were 24 bits of information, in a relation to each other that was represented in charts as well as talk. The task was to remember associated bits of information about six cultures as they existed before European contact The "scripts" introduced, elaborated and rehearsed the information in different social configurations. The planning and implementation proceeded much more smoothly, and analysis of the resulting teaching/learning process was possible.

In the second year, we used the "combination of chemicals" task (Inhelder & Piaget, 1958) with sequences of actions for making pairs

Table 2.1. *Names and tracers of the cycles reported*

Name	Tracer	Chapter
1. Electricity	None	2
2. Native Americans	24 facts about 6 cultures	7
3. Household chemicals	Patterns for combining pairs, including *intersection*	3, 5
4. Division	The *divide* step in the alogrithm	6

from a set of objects and particularly the "intersection" schema as our tracers. Intersection was a systematic and readily identifiable procedure that could be located in a variety of contexts. The analysis of this cycle is featured in Chapters 3 and 5.

Also in the second year, and reported in Chapter 6, we worked on a division cycle. The task is to divide with remainders, e.g., "5 goes into 27, 5 and 2 remaining." The tracer was "divide" as used in the children's mnemonic chant "Divide, multiply, subtract, bring down," and as encountered in the first operation for dividing a whole number by another one when the answer is not a whole number. The tracer in this case is a well-known (perhaps, notorious) culturally elaborated tool that exists externally and appears to correspond to the internal functioning of those doing division. In this cycle, we followed the teacher's lead in planning: she was the expert in knowing how novel this was for fourth graders and what sequence of sessions would provide for the repeated occurrence of the task in different guises.

From the failures and successes that we experienced in the various cycles, a methodology built around sequences of instructional tasks evolved. We knew from the start that there would be a blurry line between the task and the social organization in which it appeared. Our task/curriculum units would have to constrain our investigation of this blurry line: they would have to embody strategies for encompassing in a single system of ideas what other approaches characterize separately as the cognitive versus the social aspects of learning. We began with ideal cognitive tasks that included tracers; we tried forcing the tasks, with the assistance of elaborated scripts, into a variety of social configurations. Our major effort was to do enough work with the varying social situations so that we could specify how and why tasks appeared or disappeared, became mutilated or transformed.

Change in the process of research

As we have sketched in the sequence of experiments, and as we hope to make clear in the ensuing chapters, the analysis of the research problem that we started with developed as a result of our confrontation with the reality of the classroom. Our work was simultaneously theoretical and empirical – the findings we report are as much revisions and reinterpretations of the theory based on events in the classroom as a presentation of empirical results. Such changes in the course of research result naturally from the interactions between the initial research problems, the actual classrooms, and the developing theory. The formation of the approach outlined in this book can be summarized as a concrete example of the principles of cognitive change.

> First, *our own understandings* changed as the result of carrying out a joint activity with others who had a different analysis of our shared situation (i.e., practicing teachers).
>
> Second, there were concrete constraints from the specific domain we were all working in that increased the chances of shared understanding and decreased the chances of the task disintegrating.
>
> Third, we were not subjected to direct instruction (which in any case we would not have understood at the outset!).
>
> Fourth, this book reflects the diversity of articulations and revisions of the problem that are its history.

These features of our learning experience are familiar to most researchers who have tried to collaborate with others in order to develop new knowledge for the scientific community. They are generally absent, however, from current psychological accounts of cognitive change, which focus on individual actors. As we hope we can show, this pattern of mutual disinterest is neither accidental nor inevitable. There are systematic reasons for the psychological assumption of the individual as a unit of analysis which have been extremely important in shaping educationally focused research. If we are successful, this book will provide an alternative system based on, and illustrated by, the interactions we observed and the conflicts we experienced during our work in the classroom.

3   Making goals happen

One of our formative experiments had fourth graders working in groups of two or three at the science table mixing chemicals in test tubes. It was part of a classroom unit on "Household Chemicals" and like the lessons and activities that preceded it, the activity was carefully scripted, all the way down to the teacher's planned unobtrusiveness while the children figured out which chemicals to mix and how to record them on their worksheets. Our goal in the chemical combinations task was to create a loosely supervised isomorph of a laboratory task that the same children had already carried out individually. With data such as these we might begin to unravel the tight intertwining of cognitive and social processes.

Our method of trying to get the same task to happen in two settings, in this case, led us to an important understanding about tasks and goals. We argue in this chapter that the standard "division of labor" between researcher and subject in cognitive research tends to obscure an important feature of cognition. Specifically, experimenters have little chance to observe *how the subjects form new goals*. By comparing how the same task emerges in the two settings, we are forced to take a step back and begin to see the laboratory task as a kind of very tightly supervised instructional interaction. We are also able to take a step forward in our understanding of how in ordinary instructional interactions, children are able to come away with new understandings of the goals that can be pursued in a new situation.

The "same task" in two settings

As we discussed in Chapter 2, our goal in designing cycles was to create what cognitive psychologists call problem isomorphs.

32

In the cases we will be discussing, the isomorph comes from Inhelder and Piaget's work on formal operations. Children were asked at one time to make all the possible pairs from four stacks of differently colored cards (with pictures of movie stars on them) and at another time to make all the possible pairwise mixtures from a set of four chemicals. In our application of the problem isomorph formulation we changed not only the content (chemicals versus movie stars) but also the participant structure, i.e., the people who are responsible for the cognitive task as a social construction. We departed from the one-to-one social organization of the standard laboratory setting for cognitive research in that we had groups of children working together in the chemicals activity. We also took away, by and large, the on-line social structuring acitivity of the experimenter. The teacher, who was responsible for the chemicals versions of the problem isomorph, was instructed to walk away and busy herself with another task.

This unusual participant structure change shifted social control of the task to the little society of children. This change in social organization produced the change in the *source* of the problem that became one focal point of our work. In the one-to-one movie star situation the child was *presented* with the task of finding all the pairs of problem elements. The experimenter worked to train the child to answer the question, to follow the imperative, to act under the control of the task. In the chemicals situation, children had to *discover* the problem for themselves as they began to run out of pairs of chemicals to mix.

In the laboratory setting, we expect the task to be presented clearly to the subject. It is part of the experimenter's job. We conduct pilot studies to find out how to do this effectively; we arrange training on the task and choose criterion measures that let us know whether the subject "understands" the task that we have constructed. These procedures are certainly socially constructed. In everyday situations people are not always presented with clearly stated goals. They often have to figure out what the problem is, what the constraints are, *as well as* how to solve the problem once they have formulated it. In other words, in everyday situations people are confronted with the "whole" task. There is no experimenter responsible for doing the presentation part.

This broader conception of the whole task is important to our analyses of the transformation of a task when it is embedded in different social settings. When we look for the "same task" happening outside of the laboratory, we have to look for how the work of specifying and constraining the task is getting done and who is doing it. This kind of analysis provides us with the basis for arguing that the practical methods of maintaining control in the laboratory veil a crucial process: *formulating the task and forming the goal.*

Description of the task environments

To create examples of the "same task" in two different settings we needed a task that would have an easily analyzable and recognizable procedure, one which the children would not already know. This procedure would function as our "tracer." It would also be potentially useful to the children if they recognized that they had been confronted with the same task in some new setting.

We found an appropriately simple, but exotic, task among a set that Piaget and Inhelder (1975) used in their studies of combinations and permutations, the ability to generate all possible pairs from a set of items using stacks of differently colored chips. There is an accepted "formal operational" procedure for the systematic solution of this combinations problem which we thought was both elegant and probably beyond the capacity of our fourth graders as individual inventions. For us, the combinations task was also useful because Inhelder and Piaget (1958) studied a version of it which involved combinations of chemicals. Since the classroom teacher was already planning a unit on household chemicals, we had an opportunity to embed this well-analyzed cognitive task into the ordinary course of classroom activities.

Description of the household chemicals cycle

Managing the conjunction of our research task and the curriculum unit, i.e., appropriating classroom activity for research purposes, was not without its difficulties. For one thing, the teacher was concerned that children not come to think that it is okay to mix chemicals just to see what happens. Children might go home and begin randomly mixing the dangerous chemicals found under the kitchen sink. The chemicals combination task could lead them to do that since, in itself, it contains no larger rationale or "lesson."

Developmental psychologists normally tell children they are going to "play a little game" or give them some other isolating kind of introduction as a way of getting children to engage in the task without worrying how it will have an impact on their school grades or other parts of their lives. A classroom activity, part of a curriculum unit, cannot be introduced that way. So we developed a sequence of lessons on chemical properties as a way of placing the chemical combinations task in the context of finding out what happens when different chemicals are mixed together. We also developed a lesson on dangerous household chemicals both to meet the state curriculum expectations and to impress on the children the importance of not playing with the bottles under their kitchen sink.

The classroom unit on household chemicals consisted of five classroom events over the course of a week:

1. It began with a large-group lesson introducing the unit and particularly the notion of chemicals and substances which may be mixtures or compounds of them.
2. The next day, another large-group lesson was concerned with dangerous chemicals and how to read labels.
3. On the third day of the unit the teacher taught the set of small-group lessons which we discuss in Chapter 5.
4. The next event in the cycle consisted of two group activities which children did at a table at the back of the room without the direct supervision of the teacher. The first of these had two parts. A mystery liquids activity asked the children to identify three liquids on the basis of their interactions with starch and baking soda. A combinations of chemicals activity asked children to find out as much as they could about four chemicals by combining them with each of the other chemicals. This is the event we focus on in this chapter and describe more completely in a subsequent section.
5. A final event the next day was also a chemical combination task, directly modeled on the Piagetian task in which children had to reason about the pattern of results that occurred when each chemical and chemical combination was combined with a special indicator. The added complexity of this final task created additional problems for the children. In any case, compared with the simpler combinations task done the day before, it was not as good an isomorph of the "movie star" combinations task presented during the tutorial session which we describe in the next section of this chapter.

Two club activities followed the classroom unit. The clubs were run throughout the year by UCSD staff associated with the project. The clubs met after school or on Saturdays in the regular classroom. Two computer clubs allowed children to play computer games and use a word processor. In these clubs we tried to instantiate the combinations task by organizing a tournament in which each child had to compete with every other child. A club called the Backpack Bears met on Saturday and learned about camping equipment, cooked a backpack meal and engaged in other activities which secretly instantiated various tasks which had been built into the cycles. The activity which provided a version of the combinations task was a task in which the children were asked to figure out how many different kinds of stew could be created from a limited set of dried ingredients. Many of the children engaged in the "combinations of stew" task but the children were unconstrained in their movements around the room or orientation to the camera and consequently our videotapes failed to capture the moves in sufficient detail to permit analysis. In the computer tournament, children simply ignored the task, preferring to choose their own next opponent rather than follow a prespecified plan.

The combinations tasks

"Laboratory" version of the task. The research cycle actually began two months before the first lesson on chemicals with a tutorial concerning the combinations task which was part of a series of tests and other assessments given at the beginning of the school year. In our one-to-one tutorial situation, each child was invited into the library corner of the classroom by a researcher and was presented with stacks of little cards. Each stack of cards was a different color and bore the picture of a different TV or movie star; the child and the tutor looked over the pictures and named the stars, sometimes using the actor's name, sometimes the name of the character the actor played. To introduce the child to the task and constraints, the tutor asked the child to choose three stacks and then to make one pair, then another pair and finally a third pair, each different from the other. The tutor explained that two cards from the same stack do not count as a pair and that changing the order of the cards does not make it

a different pair: Mork and Tattoo is the same as Tattoo and Mork. The tutor picked up the pairs that had been used to demonstrate, then asked the child to choose a fourth star and she arranged the four stacks of cards in a horizontal row. She initiated the first task by asking the child to find all the ways that pairs of stars could be friends. Specifically, the child was asked to *make all the pairs of stars and none that were the same*. The child then usually went about choosing pairs of cards from the stacks and placing them in a column.

When the child had done as many pairs as s/he could, the researcher instituted a short tutorial before doing another trial of pair making. She asked the child to check to see if s/he had made all the pairs. If the child did not invent a systematic procedure for checking, the tutor suggested one, asking "Do you have all the pairs with Mork?" (if Mork were the first star on the left). Then she asked about the next star to the right. She continued asking the child to check each star until they reached the fourth star or until the child picked up the responsibility and finished checking each of the stars her/himself.

These hints were designed to give the child the idea of systematically pairing each star with every other star, so as to see whether this systematic procedure carried over to the next trial at making combinations. When the checking was finished, the pictures were put back in their piles and a fifth star was chosen. Again the child was asked to make all the possible pairs and none more than once. At this point, many of the children began by making all the pairs with the left-most star. This star was combined with each to its right. Then the second star (from the left) was combined with each to its right and so on until all the combinations were made. For children who did not arrive at this particular system of *producing* pairs, the checking procedure was repeated. But this time the tutor gave instructions that were as explicit as necessary to get the child through an entire check step by step. That is, the tutor asked about each star and its pairing with every other star in a systematic left-to-right manner. In the final trial, the child chose a sixth star and attempted to make all the possible pairs.

The "tracer" procedure. The tutorial accomplished two things. First, it acted as a pretest of the children in a typical laboratory setting on one version of the combinations task. Second, it taught the children

Table 3.1. *A "schema" for the intersection procedure*

	A	B	C	D	E
A		A&B	A&C	A&D	A&E
B			B&C	B&D	B&E
C				C&D	C&E
D					D&E

a procedure for determining that they had made all the pairs.[1] The procedure of combining each item with every other item could then act as a tracer in a later task with a different social organization. If the children later used the particular procedure we taught (and if it were reasonable to assume that the procedure would not be used except for the goal of finding all pairs), then we would have reason to think that they had identified the same task that we did.

The Piagetian analysis of this combinations procedure is useful because it is abstract enough to apply to combinations problems presented in many modes. He referred to the procedure as "intersection." As he conceived of it, the child is coordinating several series of correspondences. This can be understood as treating the single array (e.g., four stars) as if there are two dimensions that intersect. Each item on one dimension is paired with the items on the other dimension in the manner of a matrix like that shown in Table 3.1. With this matrix conception, choosing pairs follows planfully from beginning to end. All the children have to do is work through the matrix,[2] maintaining a diagonal which separates out the duplicates.[3]

---

[1] The task as formulated by the researcher was to make all the pairs *and* no duplicates. We will concentrate our discussion on the goal of getting all the pairs, which was the primary focus of the checking procedure.

[2] If the child is just checking if all the pairs are done, it is often just as easy to go, say, row by row even though checks are duplicated. In the production of pairs where duplication is not allowed, the system of dropouts is usually used so that only, say, the top half is produced.

[3] An algebraic representation is available for this formulation of the solution:

$$X = \frac{N!}{K!(N-K)!}$$

where X is the number of pairs, N is the number of items, and K is the arrangement (e.g., 2 for pairs), so that for 4 items 6 pairs can be made, for 5 items 10 pairs can be made.

It is important to realize that the behavioral display needed for the analyst to code the child as having accomplished the task does not require algebra or a matrix. Piaget and Inhelder looked for a pattern in the pair making: if all the iterations of making a pair with one member were grouped together and followed by the group of iterations with another item (e.g., 1&2, 1&3, 1&4, 2&3, 2&4, 3&4), then the child could be coded as using the conceptual matrix.

Piaget and Inhelder assumed that children who do not display the conceptual matrix typically make pairs without an orderly pattern or make patterns such as 1&2, 3&4, 2&3, 1&4. Without the matrix concept, the children cannot be certain they have all the pairs; instead, they stop when they "just can't think of" any more patterns. This endpoint is not formally specifiable; it lacks the certainty or sense of necessity found in the intersection procedure, distinguishing the processes involved as (empirical) concrete operations rather than formal (logical) operations.

It is important to our analysis to recognize that the Inhelder and Piaget intersection matrix is not the only systematic formulation of the task. An alternate analysis is represented in Table 3.2. We developed this analysis based on the sequence of acts of participants who are successful in their attempt to make all the pairs and no duplicates. A child can reach the end-point with certainty and the sense of necessity by "going twice across the row." Rather than conceiving of the items as orthogonal to themselves and hence forming a matrix, the subject with this formulation of the solution can be described as performing

Table 3.2. *The intersection procedure*

Given:	A	B	C	D	E
First move:	A&B				
Second move:	A&C				
Third move:	A&D				
Fourth move:	A&E				
Fifth move:	B&C				
Sixth move:	B&D				
Seventh move:	B&E				
Eighth move:	C&D				
Ninth move:	C&E				
Tenth move:	D&E				

recursive operations. All the child has to do is treat the first item as an anchor, pairing it with each succeeding item in the row; in the next iteration the second item in the row is treated as the anchor to be paired with the remaining succeeding items, etc.[4]

As far as we can tell, there is no way to decide between these alternate analyses of the solution.[5] The same "tracer" behavior is involved; each solution provides the subject with the sense of necessity that makes the problem an interesting one for research. One might argue that the matrix representation is more sophisticated or indicative of a higher level of development, or vice versa.

However, the difference between the representations is neutral to our claims. We are not concerned with testing the children's "operational level"; we chose the task for its usefulness as a tracer in our design. While we occasionally make use of Piagetian analyses, we are essentially taking the task outside of the theory that generated it.[6] In fact, the appearance of multiple possible analyses and the difficulty of maintaining a claim about a single resultant mental representation is consistent with the theoretical position we discuss in the next chapter.

We can consider the procedure we taught the children to be *potentially* general enough to apply to any number or any kind of items should the structure of the activity make it useful. In cognitive psychology, such an abstract and general structure would usually be called a "schema" and would be considered to be a feature of a subject's

---

[4] An arithmetic representation is available for this alternate formulation of the solution:

$$S = (N - 1) + (N - 2) + \ldots (N - N)$$

where N is the number of items and S is the number of pairs. This simple series formula accounts for making pairs with any number of items; but unlike the algebraic representation of the matrix, it cannot extend, as stated, to the making of triples or quadruples, etc. Either more formulae or a formula with a recursive calculation would be required to capture this kind of generality. Since the generalizing that we asked the children to do involved only an increase in the number of items to be *paired*, not a change in the arrangement from pairs to, say, triplets, either formalism describes the systematic behavior that Inhelder and Piaget call intersection.

[5] An experiment might be designed such that children trained to use the sequence of pairs procedure are compared with children trained to use a matrix procedure on the basis of their ability to approach the problem of making triples. On the basis of such an experiment, it would be possible to distinguish empirically the alternatives.

[6] For another discussion of Piaget's theory in relation to our approach see Newman, Riel & Martin (1983).

internal conceptualization (cf. Bartlett, 1932; Abelson, 1981; Rumelhart, 1980).[7] We will be looking for this "schema" outside of the laboratory, and we will be careful not to give it an exclusively mental status. In looking for this schema in the peer interaction setting which we describe shortly, we had to allow that it would be found as much *interpsychologically* (i.e., mediating social interactions) as *intrapsychologically* (i.e., mediating an individual's actions). Even using this tracer as a frame for comparison between the two settings, our attempt to locate the "same task" was far from straightforward.

The chemicals task. The setting with which we contrasted the movie stars version of the task looked very different. It was one lesson in the unit on household chemicals. A series of lessons and activities led up to this group version of the combinations problem, which was presented as a special work-table activity like many nonteacher led lessons. Groups of two and three children went to the back of the room where the teacher supervised some science activities, one of which involved making combinations of chemicals. Each group of children was given four beakers of liquid chemical solutions which were numbered for easy reference, a rack of test tubes, and a sheet of paper with two columns in which to record "CHEMICALS" and "WHAT HAPPENED." The four chemicals had been chosen (with the help of UCSD chemist Dr. Charles Perrin) so that each pair would produce a distinctive reaction.[8]

The written worksheet instructed the children to find out as much as they could about the chemicals by making all the combinations of two and recording the results. After getting a child to read the instructions aloud, the teacher reiterated some safety precautions and directed the children to make all the possible pairs without duplicates. The teacher then sat down at the far end of the table and busied herself with paperwork so that she could observe the children without directly supervising them. She intervened on occasion when children

[7] Recent cognitive science taking the Parallel Distributed Processing approach has reconceptualized the schema in terms of the relation between the cognitive representation and the environment, bringing cognitive science closer to a Vygotskian position. Their speculation that *external* representations mediate sequential processes is also interesting in this respect (Rumelhart et al., 1986).

[8] The chemicals were: sodium meta-bisulfate ($NaHSO_3$), Clorox bleach ($NaOCl$), copper sulfate ($CuSO_4$), potassium iodide (KI).

ran into difficulty or asked for help, but for the most part, the children worked on their own. It was thus more markedly like a peer group activity with fewer laboratory-like constraints on what was to be done or how to do it than is typically the case in cognitive experiments.

How we tried to make the "same task" happen

We went to considerable effort to give the combinations task a good chance of happening in the two settings. Most notably, in both cases a responsible adult (the researcher or teacher) stated the goal of making all the pairs at the start of the problem. These measures were not always sufficient to make the task happen even in these somewhat constrained settings, creating variability that allows us to investigate our central claims.

We anticipated difficulties in getting the task to happen in the chemicals setting because it seemed to us that the movie star activity posed far fewer practical problems. The movie star cards were just the right size for placing one pair under another in a neat and accessible column on the mat next to the child. Once a column was constructed, it was easily scanned and checked; the cards were brightly colored and the pictures were distinctive.

The chemicals were much harder to manage physically. They had to be transferred from beakers to test tubes and once a pair was combined in the tube there was no automatically available visual record of which ones had been put in.

If the children were unable to mix and keep track of the chemicals we could hardly expect them to attend to the task of getting *all* the combinations. Our solution was to set up a prior lesson (described in more detail in Chapter 5) in which the children had to place a chemical solution and a chemical indicator into a test tube and record the results on a form, just like the one which was to be used later in the combinations of chemicals task. We also numbered the beakers so that the children would have a familiar, ordered reference system with which to work. The recording sheets and the numbers on the beakers provided not only an "external memory" for each child but also common reference points for the groups who were expected to be working together.

In spite of the long list of differences between the two situations, there was still an important way in which they were the same. In both settings the intersection procedure – our tracer – was potentially useful if the children accepted *our* notion of the task. At the same time, the nature of our enterprise required that we take some chances. In the chemicals activity we could not direct the children to use the tracer or force the task to happen. The lack of teacher/researcher direction was the crucial difference we wanted to maintain. If, despite that difference, we were still able to locate the tracer, we would have an anchor point from which to begin an analysis of the "same task" in two different settings.

Comparing the two settings

We started out assuming that we had problem isomorphs in the ordinary sense, i.e., participants in the two settings would have a common abstract goal. We knew that this assumption would be difficult to warrant, but we wanted to push the standard approach as far as it would go, to discover how it broke down. The problems we ran into forced the alternative analysis which we will describe below.

Our initial attempt to code performance

Once the videotapes were collected, we started out to *code* the events for occurrences of our tracer, e.g., we classified the behaviors according to our *a priori* task analysis. Once coded, we could simply, run a statistical test to see if performance on the two tasks was correlated.

In coding both tasks we were looking for any instance of a child going through a sequence like 1&2, 1&3, 1&4, 2&3, and so on, i.e., a sequence in which each item is paired with every other item in a systematic way we could recognize. The sequence could be either a complete run-through of the procedure or a fragment of the procedure (e.g., all the 2s: 2&1 2&3 2&4). We used a three-point scale: "1" meant no fragments of the procedure were found, "2" meant that some fragments of the procedure were found, and "3" meant that the child produced at least one complete run-through of the procedure. Where a sequence was produced collaboratively by two children, we credited each child with a partial sequence.

In the movie star task, only 3 children out of 27 started using the intersection procedure on the first trial. But after the tutor provided the prompts during the "checking" phase (after the child's independent effort), 17 children used a complete run-through of the procedure, and 4 others used it partially, in the second or third trial. In the chemicals task, the coding credited only 4 children with a complete run-through of the procedure, although 8 others did at least one set (e.g., all the 4s). In statistical terms, the conclusion from such a coding approach is a relatively low correlation between performance in the two settings (Kendall's tau is .37). One child performed better in the peer interaction chemicals setting: The child did a full run-through of the procedure in the chemicals task but produced only a fragment in the last trial of the movie star task. The opposite pattern was more common, however. Five children used the tracer procedure in the movie stars but not at all in the chemicals.

We might also take these results to indicate that, in some sense, the movie star task was easier; the chemical materials may have been too difficult to manage physically and too unfamiliar. But, for the current discussion, there is a more important sense in which the movie star task was easier. *It was far easier for us to code.* For one thing, we knew what part of the sequence was relevant to code. We focused on just those testing trials where the child was asked to produce the pairs from 4, 5, or 6 stacks of stars on his/her own. In fact, we went to some effort to train our tutor not to help the child in any way during these response slots. In contrast, the intersection sequences were located at various points in the chemicals activity, both as a physical accomplishment and in the children's talk about what pairs had, or had not, been done. Also, children were not isolated from each other as sources of help. The intersection sequences which appeared during the chemical task were often collaborative productions which were difficult to code in anything but an *ad hoc* way as an independent achievement (our solution was to give each participant credit for only a partial sequence).

These differences provide us with crucial points of comparison. The coder's problems are symptomatic of differences for the participants (including the teacher and researcher) in what the task was and how the work got done.

Locating the tracer in the chemicals activity

The chemicals activity presented us with two kinds of difficulty: (1) knowing where to find the tracer in the course of the children's activity, and (2) knowing to whom we should attribute the procedure.

Finding the tracer. Since we had set up the chemicals activity to resemble Inhelder and Piaget's task, we initially approached the scoring as they had. We examined the sequence of pairs the children mixed. We sought to determine if the children would use the tracer procedure to produce the pairs of chemicals as they had produced the pairs of movie stars in the tutorial, for example, starting out with 1&2 and proceeding to do all the pairs with 1 and so on through the six possible pairs. This *never* happened. Instead, the groups of children started with whatever pair was most convenient or was "thought of first" (for lack of a better description). The sequence of pairs either manifested no pattern at all or took on patterns such as, for example, "doing the middle then the ends" of the row of beakers. As can be seen in the protocols reported below, these patterns were not usually produced as part of a single, coherent sequence by the children. One common pattern started with 1&2 then 3&4 when the two children who were part of the group but working independently each took the two closest beakers. If it appeared, the intersection procedure arose first in the *talk* among the children. When the children could not think up another pair that had to be done, they would discuss the written record or would consult one another's memory. That is, they used the procedure as a method for *checking*. This sequence repeats our observation in the movie star tutorial; in these instances, however, the children initiated the checking.

A group composed of Thomas, Candy and Elvia provides a good example of this process. At the beginning of the task they settled on a turn-taking order which they maintained throughout. During a turn, one child both mixed the chemicals and recorded the results. This does not mean, however, that the children worked alone; many of the decisions about what to mix and how to describe the result were made after extensive discussion. At each new turn, one child chose a pair

Elvia
Tom s
Candy

Chemicals	What Happens
2 and 3	turd green
3 & 4	turned brown yellow
1 & 2	Hot
2 3 4	yallow and warm
4 & 1	turned clear
1 & 3	turned yellow green

Figure 3.1. Thomas, Candy, and Elvia's record sheet.

and the other children checked it against the record. The sequences of choices followed no apparent order through the six possible pairs and, until the last two pairs, the children had no difficulty thinking up a new pair that had yet to be done. The last two pairs were also arrived at without apparent system but with growing concern about finding more to do. The record sheet is reproduced in Figure 3.1.

After Candy's second turn, the six pairs were done. However, the children were not aware of this, as this record of their action and talk indicates:

> Elvia takes an empty test tube from the rack, preparing to mix another pair.
>
> With a sigh, Elvia says, "I don't know what color to USE now..." Thomas suggests 2&4 but Elvia finds it on the worksheet. Thomas jokingly suggests 2&2 and Candy suggests 2&4 again. Thomas thinks of 2&1 but finds it has been done.

Candy suggests 4&2. There is a mild rebuke from Thomas that it is the same as 2&4.

Elvia comes up with 4&3 but Candy finds it has been done.

Elvia suggests 4&1 and Candy recalls that she did it.

At that point Thomas says, "There's no more."

Candy thinks of 3&1 and Elvia thinks of 3&2.

But they find both of those on the written record, too.

Then Elvia suggests 3&4.

At that point Thomas says "Wait a minute, kay, we got, okay we got all the 1s."

He moves his finger up the record sheet and hesitates when he finds only two of them but then finds the third.

Candy says, "All the ones with 2? 2&3."

She pauses and then says, "They don't have 4&1," but Thomas points it out.

At that moment the teacher asks, "You have them all?"

And Thomas answers, "Yep."

The intersection sequence *can* be recovered from this interaction. For almost a minute, the three children named off pairs with 4 until Candy moved to 3&1 after which Elvia named the other pairs with 3. Then Thomas looked for all the 1s and Candy suggested looking for the 2s. The order is not "perfect" but as a group they manage to check through all the pairs with each of the chemicals.[9]

Finding our tracer, the intersection procedure, in the talk among the children as they set about to check their work showed us that at least some of the children indexed the "same task" in the new setting. But the task they found there was not an isomorph of the one that the tutor had trained them to solve on their own in the last independent production trial in the movie star tutorial. Rather, what

---

[9] Several groups of children produced this sort of sequence. Usually these checks would not follow strictly the 1 to 4 order but would skip around, partially depending on the order in which the combinations were recorded on the worksheet. For example, a child would search for all the 4s by reading down the worksheet and naming off all the pairs with 4 as they were encountered. This strategy has the advantage of making the search of the record more efficient although it means the memory load is increased because the child must keep in mind which of the pairs with 4 have been found.

the children found in the new setting was the task as it had been se-
quenced in the activities that *the child and tutor* had constructed together. The tracer was first introduced during the movie star tutorial
in the tutor–child *checking* interaction. The tutor motivated the procedure for the child, as a way the child could make sure he had all
the pairs. In the chemicals task, the procedure was again motivated by
the need to find out if there were any more pairs to do. But this time,
the children motivated the task themselves rather than having it suggested by the tutor.

Determining who did it. We expected difficulty of attribution in coding. Because the children were not working alone we could not always
attribute the procedure to a single child (see McDermott & Tylbor,
1983). In the example of Thomas, Elvia and Candy the sequence was
made up of contributions from all the children and no child carried
out the whole strategy independently. The intersection schema thus
regulated the interaction among the children as part of the context
that regulates the individuals' actions.

It should not be thought that peer collaboration in the chemicals
activity automatically obscured individual accomplishment. Some
children divided the labor in such a way as to make it possible to attribute the schema to an individual. In one case, two boys, Mike and
Jorge, who were best friends, collaborated closely. Jorge writes down
the numbers of the beakers as Mike mixes. They exchange roles after
each pair is recorded, so that Mike records while Jorge mixes. They
alternate turns through the six possible combinations although the
ordering shows no apparent pattern to the choice of chemicals they
mixed. See Figure 3.2. As the following record shows, the intersection procedure again emerges *post hoc* as a checking procedure.

> Mike takes out a test tube to begin another combination but stops to
> look over at the record.
>
> Mike starts a checking sequence at 1&2 and from there continues
> through the whole sequence in canonical order, ending with 3&4.
> (This is not the sequence of discovery recorded on the printed
> page.)
>
> While he is naming the chemicals, he points to the numbered
> beakers which remain in a neat array.

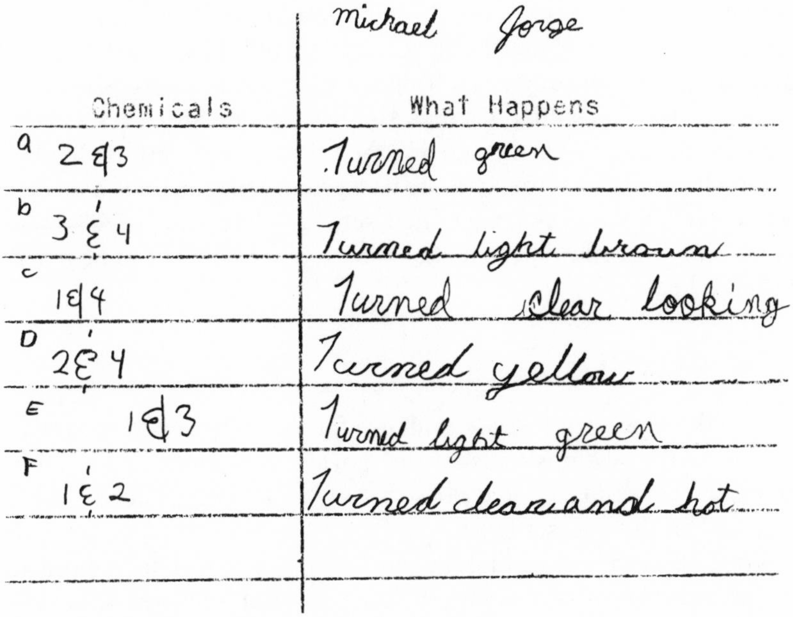

	michael	Jorge
Chemicals	What Happens	
a 2 & 3	Turned green	
b 3 & 4	Turned light brown	
c 1 & 4	Turned clear looking	
D 2 & 4	Turned yellow	
E 1 & 3	Turned light green	
F 1 & 2	Turned clear and hot	

Figure 3.2. Mike and Jorge's record sheet.

Jorge, in the meantime, studies the record, finding the combinations Mike is naming.

Mike and Jorge divided up the checking roles just as they had divided up the roles in producing and recording the chemicals. One dealt with the chemicals while the other dealt with the writtern record. Because Mike was the one to name off the sequence of pairs, we do not hesitate to attribute the schema to Mike. But the schema also regulates the interaction between the two boys. Thus we find again that the intersection schema is not just, or even primarily, an *internal* knowledge structure. It is also importantly locatable *in the interaction among the children*. It is, in Vygotsky's terminology, an *interpsychological*, cognitive process.

In an important sense the process of constructing the intersection procedure was always a social accomplishment in all the settings we studied. When we look back at the tutorial it is clear that the creation of the protected system in which the procedure could be carried out cleanly was a piece of collaborative social organization. Such organizational support for problem solving is a systematic feature of settings organized for individual testing. But when individual assessment provides the motive for the activity, the organizational efforts tend to go unnoticed because they are the background that enables us to see the "data." In the less constrained setting, Mike and Jorge's marvelous bit of organization to make visible similar "data" can be better appreciated.

Locating the "same task"

While we can provide evidence for the existence of our tracer in many of the sessions (most of the movie star sessions and some of the chemical sessions), what does that say about the existence of the same *task* in the two settings?

When we set about coding the movie star session we felt confident that we knew how to specify the task so that what we were coding was the child's performance on the task. We identified the task with the goal "make all the pairs" and with the constraints specified in the instructions, both of which were stated by the researcher just before the child began forming pairs of movie stars. The researcher was careful not to give any information until it was clear that the child was not going to make any more pairs on his/her own. The slot between the researcher's instructions and the child's negative answer to the question, "Can you make any more?" provided easy access to the *individual* child's use of the intersection procedure. We felt confident that we could say that when introduced to the task of making all the pairs some children used the procedure or used it partially and some children didn't use it at all. Our struggle with the chemicals setting, however, led us eventually to question those assumptions.

In the chemicals activity it became clear to us that the children, when they started out, were *not* doing the task. The teacher told them to make all the pairs before they started. But for two important reasons there was no evidence that they were trying to make *all* the pairs. First, the children were clearly pursuing other goals. Second, they were not using the intersection procedure (or, apparently, any other systematic procedure) for making all the pairs.

Doing other tasks. If the children were not doing the task of producing all possible pairs, as we defined and sought to construct it, what were they doing? The teacher's instructions at the beginning of the episode stated, but did not emphasize, the goal of getting *all* the pairs. She emphasized the problem of finding out about the chemicals by seeing how they reacted with other chemicals. The reactions that were produced by different chemical combinations were fascinating to the children, and they were generally interested in the problem of describing the results and writing them down.

Tracy's approach illustrates the common interest in the chemicals themselves. Instead of using the numbers on the beakers, he used the actual chemical names printed on the beakers. His record sheet is shown in Figure 3.3. After mixing Clorox from beaker 2 with copper sulfate from beaker 3, he was excited and described in detail the blue-green and brown dotted reaction. He appeared to want to pursue reactions with "copper." His partners, who were working together, tried to trade their beaker 4 for his beaker 3. He looked up from the worksheet to object: "I got copper!" His partners were attempting to choose their next pair with reference to the worksheet so as to avoid duplication of pairs. Tracy's criterion for a next step appeared to depend on the visual effects associated with a particular chemical.

Not doing intersection. Children who do not do the intersection or some other systematic procedure, yet succeed in producing pairs of chemicals, find the pairs "empirically" according to Inhelder and Piaget's original analysis. This means that the children think up a "next pair" by some means other than the intersection procedure and look to see whether it has been done. In this case, the children have no way of knowing when they are finished except that they cannot think of any more.

The Piagetian analysis suggested that a child who was making pairs empirically was doing the *same actions* (mixing pairs, writing the results on the worksheet) but was not doing the *same task* as a child who was guided by the endpoint that the researcher had in mind. For the child not using intersection, the task is like a request to jump as high as you can. How high a person can jump is an empirical issue and the outcome differs for different children. For the child who could use it, the idea of intersection provided a definite goal; if achieved, the solu-

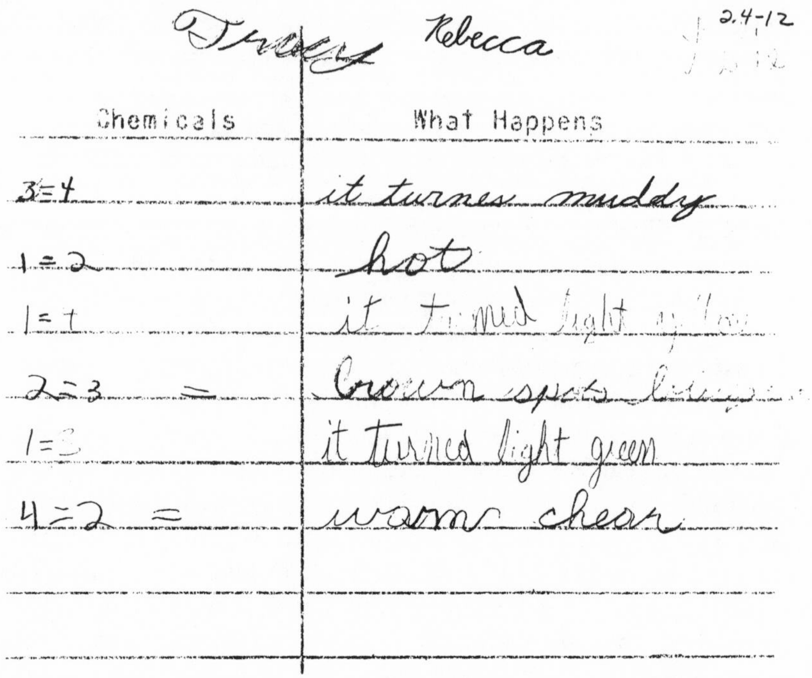

Figure 3.3. Tracy, Rebecca, and Leslie's record sheet.

tion is general and independent of the particular child and particular times. In the chemicals activity the teacher's statement of the task goal, "Make all the pairs you can," was not acted upon as the teacher and researcher had in mind. The task as the teacher and researchers understood it happened only after the children themselves formulated the goal of finding all the pairs for each other, when they tried to think of more pairs to make.

Reevaluating the evidence for the task in the tutorial. Tracy's comments about the chemical reactions with copper give us a kind of information that was almost never available in the movie star tutorials. The chemicals activity was loosely enough constrained that alternative tasks were socially permissible. We can notice that children were not doing the task because we can find them talking about doing other tasks. In the tutorials, on the contrary, little action and talk were allowed that were not about pair-making. Tracy, for example, starts the second trial (with five stars) by making a *row* of cards. We have no idea what he might have been trying to do, what his "own" task was, because he was immediately "corrected" by the researcher and told to make pairs.

The strict enforcement of pair-making in the tutorial made it difficult to notice that some children were not doing the task of making *all the pairs*. Differences in the pattern of pair placements did not stand out as indicating a different goal because they were not accompanied by other behavioral evidence that the children were doing some other specifiable task. All the constraints allowed us to assume that the children in the movie star activity were all doing the same task, differing in their cognitive activity only insofar as some were using intersection to do "it," while others were failing.

The fact that we have used the Inhelder–Piaget analysis as a foil should not blind us to the advantage that it has. Their analysis of task performance already implied that some children (those approaching it empirically) were not doing their task. It is, therefore, a more powerful analysis than many laboratory task analyses which cannot distinguish between doing poorly and not doing the task at all.

The analytic weakness of the tutorial setting for clarifying this issue can be seen when we turn to Inhelder and Piaget's claim about a transitional level of performance between "empirical" and "intersection," where children produced patterns that they called "juxtaposition" sequences (doing the ends and then the middle, e.g., 1&2, 3&4, 1&4, 2&3, and so on). They described these sequences as a "search for a system," implying that the child understood the task and was searching for a solution. Despite the plausibility of the analysis, when such sequences occur in the tutorial setting we cannot tell whether or not the child is doing the task.

In the chemicals activity, however, we have clear evidence that some of these juxtaposition sequences were produced while the children were *not* doing the task. For example, when Tracy, Leslie and Rebecca start out, Tracy takes 1&2 while Leslie and Rebecca work together on 3&4. When they finish their respective mixtures, Tracy offers his 1 for their 3 and mixes 2&3, while the girls mix 1&4. When the girls finish their mixture, Rebecca checks the record and decides to do 1&3, so they trade their 4 for Tracy's 3. These trades result in a complete juxtaposition sequence: 1&2, 3&4, 2&3, 1&4, 2&4 and 1&3. But, there is no evidence that the children had the goal of producing the pattern, that they were "searching for a system." There is evidence that the juxtaposition pattern was a result of peer negotiation, the girls on one side and Tracy and his lovely copper on the other.

When the conditions of negotiation get stringent, when everyone wants to make another mixture but many of the possible mixtures have already been made, then the children are motivated to find out if there are any pairs left to do. The way to find that out, of course, is to see if they have "made all the pairs that can be made." Furthermore, when the goal of finding if they have all the pairs does come into the Tracy, Leslie and Rebecca interaction, we find that Rebecca uses a well formed intersection procedure to reach it. She doesn't try the juxtaposition strategy at all, even though it could be retrieved from the written record of the group's prior actions. In this respect, the un-constrained setting provided us with better information about task performance than did the laboratory setting. *The constraints of the laboratory obscured whether or not some subjects were doing the task.*

The original coding scheme must be drastically reinterpreted. We can now see that most of the children in the first and second trials of the movie star task may not have been doing the task at all. Scoring a low "1" for no intersection may simply be an indication of not doing the task. The coding of the chemicals activity is also rendered prob-lematic. None of the children started out doing the task. For those who finally did engage the task, their achievement went beyond the individual achievement of any child in the tutorial because they *discovered* the task on their own.

Learning about the goal

We designed the movie stars situation in part as an indi-vidualized assessment situation and in part as a tutorial to create the procedure we wanted to use later as our tracer. The part of the tu-torial during which we taught the checking procedure was designed to make use of dynamic assessment (cf. Chapter 5 for a more complete discussion of dynamic assessment). In the procedure we used, the tutor started out the checking tutorial giving as much help as the child needed to carry out the systematic check. But as the tutorial progressed, the tutor began giving less and less help until the child was on his own.

Following Vygotsky's theoretical formulation, we would expect tasks to be found first in the interaction between expert and novice and later in the novice's independent activity. We take this to mean that the novice not only lacked the skills necessary to carry out the task independently, but, more importantly, did not initially understand the goal. In order for development to occur, the expert must ensure that the task itself occur in the interaction between the expert and novice. We want to suggest that our teaching not only provided most of the children with the intersection procedure, it also gave them the goal of finding *all* the pairs. That is, teaching the procedure in a Vygotskian manner introduced the children to the task in such a way that the goal *and* the procedure were simultaneously internalized in the course of the interaction.[10] Examples from the tutorial and the chemicals activity suggest how this internalization process might happen.

In the movie star tutorial, the children first produced a column of pairs, as many as they could, and then the tutor began teaching the checking strategy. The conversation at this point was important. The tutor asks, "How do you know you have all the pairs?" The child usually answers vaguely or, like Tracy, with a hint of frustration, "I can't think of any more." The tutor then asks, "Could you check to see if you have all the pairs?" The child usually says little and the tutor says, "Well, I have a way to check. Do you have all the pairs with Mork (or the first star on the left)?" From there she proceeds through the checking procedure, allowing the child to take over more and more as they go along.

The tutor's question, "How do you know you have all the pairs?" *presupposes* that the child was trying to get all the pairs. This may have been a false presupposition but it was strategically useful (Gearhart &

---

[10] This is not *always* the case. More than one procedure can achieve the same goal and if the child knows one procedure and is just learning another, he may not have to relearn the goal. The relationship between procedures and goals is complex. See Lawler (1981) for an interesting case study where two procedures are learned and only under tuition does it become apparent that they serve the same goal.

Newman, 1980; Stone & Wertsch, 1984; McDermott & Tylbor, 1983). The question treated the child's column of pairs *as if* it had been produced in an attempt to get all the pairs. The tutor then invoked the intersection procedure as a means to fix up the child's "failed attempt to produce all the pairs." In the terminology we adopt in this book, she appropriated the child's independent pair-making, making it a part of an example of how to achieve the stated goal. It appears that when their own "empirical" production of pairs was *retrospectively* interpreted in terms of the intersection schema, children began to learn the researcher's meaning of "all the pairs" and thereby discovered the goal.

This retrospective appropriation process was also seen at the end of the chemicals activity. The teacher always checked when the children thought they had finished and attempted to elicit a rationale for their thinking. Like the tutor-experimenter, the teacher was working with a concrete set of already produced pairs which were not necessarily produced by the children using the intersection procedure. In the chemicals task, far more than in the movie star activity, the researcher's task completely disappeared from the scene in many cases. The teacher's questions at the end brought the task back into the interaction. Her discussion demonstrated to the children how their work could be understood as doing *the teacher's* task.

In an important sense, the tutor and teacher were treating the child's production *as if* it were an attempt (sometimes poorly executed) to achieve an agreed-upon goal. In education, such assumptions may be a useful way of importing the goal into the teacher–child interaction and from there into the child's independent activity. Our original coding scheme also treated many of the children's productions *as if* they were the products of poor strategies for getting all the pairs. In psychology, such overinterpretations can be dangerously misleading. Children are scored as doing poorly when in fact they are not doing the task in the first place.

Same tasks and whole tasks

We can make some progress by collecting several problems into one: the problem of whether we can locate the "same task" in different settings, the problem of whether the child is doing the task at all, and the problem of how children learn about tasks. All of these are related. Children can start out in an interaction with a tutor without doing the task that the tutor specifies; as the tutor appropriates the child's other-task oriented behaviors, the child learns what the task really is; but in settings where there is no tutor, the "same task" must have a different genesis.

Earlier in this chapter we introduced the notion of the "whole task." We can now give it more specification. *A "whole task" is a task considered in the context of the activity which motivates and constrains it.* In some settings (like the laboratory, the classroom, or whenever there is a hierarchical division of labor), the task may not be under an actor's individual control. In such cases, the child's "whole task" may bear no useful relations to the educational goals of the teacher or the research goals of the experimenter. If the tutor's appropriation of the child's behavior is successful, the child's whole task disappears, as the adult's task appears to motivate and constrain the child's actions.

In other settings, the actors have more control over the activity and it, in turn, constrains their actions. If a task of interest to a researcher or a teacher occurs, it is from the very beginning the "whole task" of the acting subject. This was what we saw happen in the chemicals activity. The children wanted to mix more pairs of chemicals so they tried to figure out if they had done them all. Finding all the pairs was not a task which was presented to them by somebody else; it followed from the concrete situation in which they were engaged. It was motivated, in the sense of the word used in formal argumentation, i.e., it was necessitated by sequentially prior and conceptually relevant actions with the beakers and their classmates. It was the obvious next step to take to achieve their goals.

In standard laboratory practice, where it is necessary to have as complete control as possible over the subjects, subjects are not called upon to control the activity, to motivate the same "whole task" as the experimenter has motivated. They are required to merely act *as if* the task motivates their solution to the goal prepared by the experimenter. They, themselves, are not required to prepare the goal, to motivate the task. This is not to say that whole tasks are not part of the social interaction in the laboratory. The subject may be very much aware that the researcher has goals which are the motivation for getting the subject to do the task; but the subject often assumes that it is not necessary, perhaps not even proper, for him or her to understand the context of this activity. In short, there is always a "whole task," but standard laboratory cognitive tasks are organized so that there is a particular division of labor such that the subject is often confronted with the solution part alone.

In tutorials and in laboratories, we can see subjects solving problems but not finding them; giving answers which fit the questions, but not being responsible for the genesis of the questions; being constrained by the experimenter's prepared goals and acting within the conditions that the experimenter's motivation dictates. The task is, in large measure, the experimenter's, shaped by his or her discipline and his or her interactions on-line. In other settings, the actors control whether or not the task will be found to be solved; their ongoing activity is the genesis of the question and the answer; the same history that prepares the goals and the conditions for solving the problem produces the solution. Rather than seeing the task out of school and out of the laboratory as a deformed version of the original, we have a way to see the partial nature of the tasks which laboratory science can make happen.

Very often for children, goals originate in interaction with adults, as we observe in instructional interactions. In less constrained settings, children may hold more to their own goals, as we saw in the computer clubs. For example, when we tried to create a combinations task by organizing a tournament in which each child had to play every other child, the children simply ignored the structure and managed to choose their own next play partner. *But even in cases where the child's goal is not a result of adult appropriation, goals are suggested and constrained by material and social circumstances.* In the chemicals combinations task, when the children found the goal of determining they had all the pairs, the goal arose from the whole task they were engaged in. In the computer club tournament, the children's goals of playing computer games with their friends, which eclipsed the researcher's goal of creating a combinations task, arose from the social opportunities presented by the club and the computer games. These are examples of the *children's* active appropriation of available cultural resources. The appropriation process is reciprocal, and cognitive change occurs within this mutually constructive process. While instructional interactions favor the role associated with the teacher, we cannot lose sight of the continually active role of the child.

4   Basic concepts for discussing cognitive change

"Cognitive change" may be an unwieldy expression. We use it to characterize a process involving a dialectical interaction between the social world and the changing individual. Neither of the more common alternatives, learning and development, captures the phenomenon we are interested in. Nor do we see cognitive change as a higher level category such that older notions of learning and development will reappear as subtopics under cognitive change. In the process that we call cognitive change, we want to include the notions of restructuring, invention and directionality that development implies without taking on the exclusively individual, internal character that usually goes with notions of development.

Creating a new term is a way to signal that old phenomena are being reconceptualized with a different kind of theory. *One important difference is that the individual is not the most useful unit of analysis.* The shift in theoretical perspective that we are proposing raises several deep problems about what we are looking at: what *are* the units of analysis? how do we understand cognitive representations? and what does change move toward?

When we began our work together in 1978, Vygotsky's *Mind in Society* had just been published, initiating a resurgence of interest in his theory in the United States. Vygotsky's sociohistorical approach was of great interest to us because it treats the social environment for learning in a principled way as part of the process of cognitive change rather than as an unanalyzed force impinging on the individual organism. Our project gave us an opportunity to work through a synthesis of this approach with our understandings of cognitive development, discourse analysis and learning theories. Since 1978 several important volumes have appeared in this tradition including

59

Leont'ev's *Problems in the Development of the Mind* (1981), Luria's *The Making of Mind* (1979), retranslations of Vygotsky's *Thought and Language* (1986, 1987) as well as collections of essays edited by Wertsch (1981, 1985, 1986), Rogoff & Lave (1984) and Rogoff & Wertsch (1984). Our own discussions can be found in LCHC (1982, 1983), Griffin & Cole (1984) and Newman, Riel & Martin (1983). With all this activity, this chapter can afford to be relatively short, focusing only on the concepts which are central to the presentation in this book.

A most fundamental tenet of Vygotsky's theory is the integration of the "internal" and the "external." His psychology is not just about the mind nor just about the externally specifiable stimulus-response relations. It is about the dialectic between the inter- and the intra-psychological and the transformations of one into another. Mind becomes externalized by a culture in its tools, such as written language and social institutions. Cognitive change involves internalizations and transformations of the social relations in which children are involved, including the cultural tools which mediate the interactions among people and between people and the physical world. Our understanding of the basis for a cognitive science of education falls under six main topics each deriving from this basic tenet. The first concerns the zone of proximal development (ZPD). The second concerns the interaction between people with different points of view on the same situation and the *appropriation* of one view by the other, leading to cognitive change. Third, we discuss the problem of discontinuity in cognitive change as it relates to what is referred to as "Fodor's paradox." Fourth, our reconceptualization of change leads us to work with a different kind of unit of analysis. Fifth, along with a different unit of analysis comes a different way of viewing "internal representations." Finally, we discuss the directionality and endpoint of change.

Zone of proximal development

The concept of a "zone of proximal development" (ZPD) is taken from two sources in Vygotsky's writings: first, the well known *Thought and Language* and second, an essay called "The Interaction Between Learning and Development" which appeared in a collection of essays entitled *Mental Development of Children and the Process of Learning* published in Moscow in 1935 and reprinted in *Mind in Society* in 1978.[1] ZPD has been most often discussed in the context of a psychological test of mental ability. Here Vygotsky defined the zone as the difference between the level of problem difficulty that the child could engage in independently and the level that could be accomplished with adult help (Vygotsky, 1978). More generally, the concept refers to an interactive system within which people work on a problem which at least one of them could not, alone, work on effectively. Cognitive change takes place within this zone, where the zone is considered both in terms of an individual's developmental history and in terms of the support structure created by the other people and cultural tools in the setting. Methodologically, cognitive change can be observed as children pass through or work within the zone. We will use the more general interpretation of ZPD in these discussions, referring to the zone as a location – in the teacher–child interaction – in which new understandings can arise.

In Chapter 3, we illustrated a dyadic ZPD, the movie star tutorial, which we created quite specifically for research assessment. ZPD is a more general phenomenon which can often be observed when two or more people with unequal expertise are jointly accomplishing a task. This may occur in classrooms, apprenticeship settings, as well as in noninstructional settings such as mother–child interaction and children's play. Chapters 5 and 6 show the ZPD in small group lessons. Chapter 7, with a broader stroke, views a ZPD extended in time.

The concept of ZPD was developed within a theory that assumes that higher, distinctively human, psychological functions have sociocultural origins. The activities that constitute a zone *are* the social origins referred to; when cognitive change occurs not only *what* is carried out among participants, but *how* they carry it out appears again as an independent psychological function that can be attributed to the novice. That is, the culturally mediated interaction among the people in the zone is internalized, becoming a new function of the individual. Another way to say it is that the interpsychological becomes also intrapsychological.

[1] The Russian term is "zona blizaishevo razvitiya," literally "zone of nearest development," where nearest is used colloquially in such expressions as "I'll call you in the nearest future" by Russian speakers.

The notion of an interpsychological cognitive object can at first appear somewhat mysterious to cognitive scientists concerned only with internal representations. The notion is more commonplace in sociological or sociolinguistic analyses where there is a concern with constructions that are not reducible to the individual psyche. Cognitive science approaches tend to reduce social phenomena to internal representations. Without denying the importance of individual representations (or the difficulties intrinsic to determining their form), the sociocultural approach focuses on the *transformations* between the interpsychological and the intrapsychological. The analysis of social events involving negotiation between participants with different understandings or analyses of the situation becomes a necessary part of work taking this approach.

Within a ZPD, objects do not have a unique analysis. An object such as a poem, a chart or a spoken concept may be understood very differently by the child and by the teacher. Likewise, the same speech act may be interpreted quite differently. But these differences need not cause "trouble" for the teacher or the child or the social interaction; the participants can act *as if* their understandings are the same. At first, this systematic vagueness about what an object "really is" may appear to make cognitive analysis impossible. However, it now appears to us that this looseness is just what is needed to allow change to happen when people with differing analyses interact. It is also the key element for the process we call "appropriation."

Appropriation

A key concept for explaining how congnitive change can happen is suggested by a distinction made by Vygotsky's colleague, Leont'ev (1981). While accepting the fundamental notion put forth by Piaget that children actively construct their knowledge through interaction with the environment, Leont'ev replaces Piaget's concept of "assimilation" with the concept of "appropriation." With this distinction he moves from a biologically oriented metaphor to a sociohistorical one.

For Leont'ev, the objects in the child's world have a social history and functions that are not discovered through the child's unaided explorations. The usual function of a hammer, for example, is not understood by exploring the hammer itself (although the child may discover some facts about weight and balance). The child's appropriation of culturally devised "tools" comes about through involvement in culturally organized activities in which the tool plays a role. Some tools are quite different from hammers, like the mother tongue a child is exposed to or the number system and operations on numbers used in homes, businesses and schools, but the basic principle remains.

While Leont'ev preserves Piaget's fundamental insight that children have their own structured system of activity, he emphasizes the fact that they cannot and need not reinvent the artifacts that have taken millenia to evolve in order to appropriate such objects into their own system of activity. The child has only to come to an understanding that is adequate for using the culturally elaborated object in the novel life circumstances he encounters. The appropriation process is always a two-way one. The tool may also be transformed, as it is used by a new member of the culture; some of these changes may be encoded in the culturally elaborated tool, as the current sociohistorical developments allow.

Our particular interest in education leads us to notice that the teacher reciprocally applies the process of appropriation in the instructional interactions. In constructing a ZPD for a particular task, the teacher incorporates children's actions into her own system of activity. We saw this process in operation in Chapter 3 in the movie star and chemical combinations tasks where the tutor or teacher used the children's production of pairs "as if" they had been produced with the goal the teacher had in mind. This kind of appropriation is a pervasive feature of instructional interactions; Chapters 6 and 7 further illustrate its power.

Just as the children do not have to know the full cultural analysis of a tool to begin using it, the teacher does not have to have a complete analysis of the children's understanding of the situation to start using their actions in the larger system. The children's actions can function within two different understandings of the significance of the task: the child's and the teacher's. Both are constrained by sociohistorical understandings of the activity setting in which they are interacting. The fact that any action can always have more than one analysis makes cognitive change possible. Children can participate in an activity that is more complex than they can understand, producing "performance before competence," to use Cazden's (1981) phrase. While in the ZPD of the activity, the children's actions get interpreted within the system being constructed with the teacher. Thus the child is exposed to the teacher's understanding without necessarily being directly taught.

The appropriation process assumes that for any particular episode involving a novice and an expert, the novice's psychological functions constitute an organized system that permits the novice to form some notion of what the episode is going to be about. But there is no assumption that all the parties involved in a ZPD have the *same* notion of what is going to happen. In fact, the "entering" organization of functions that carries a child into an educational zone may not map at all closely onto the interactions that organize behavior within the zone. The slogan "start where the child is" holds in an unusual way, given ZPDs and the process of appropriation. The teacher must find a way to enlist all the different children so that they participate in the activity; so going to "where they are" happens in a sense. The children are making whatever sense they can (McDermott, 1976) of the activity, so they are certainly "there." But if the educational activity is successful, the teacher and the children all act as if the children are "somewhere else." That other "place" is where they could be *if* their acts are appropriated and *if* the children appropriate the activities and tools of others that cohabit in the ZPD. It is somewhat paradoxical: for a lesson to be needed, in say, division, it must be presumed that the children cannot do division; but, for the lesson to work, the presumption is that whatever the children are doing can become a way of doing division!

Two important points derive from this general character of appropriation, each of which attests to the existence of creativity in the ZPD, to the indefiniteness of what Caryl Emerson has called the "dialogue with the child's future." First, a great variety of systems of cognitive functioning may be appropriate (and appropriatable) entry points into a given zone, such that there is no simple mapping from adult system onto child system. Second, children who may be similar with respect to their entering cognitive systems may enter zones containing very different interpsychological systems, so that there is also no simple mapping between entering child system and resultant child system.

Continuity, discontinuity and Fodor's paradox

Here the sociohistorical school departs significantly from other developmental approaches. The child's new system of organization is seen to be continuous with the prior interpsychological system represented by interactions in the zone. It is discontinuous with the system that the child displayed prior to entering the zone. The relation between steps in an individual's independent development is not immediate, but rather is mediated by the social situations in which the individual participates.

For example, in the movie star task, many children adopted the intersection strategy, which had been performed interactively in the checking tutorial, after first solving the problem "empirically" or by "juxtaposition." We noted that the juxtaposition strategy did not appear as a step in a developmental sequence. Children's performance changed from either of the nonintersection strategies to the intersection strategy after intersection was done interactively in the ZPD of the tutorial. There was a clear continuity between the ZPD and the later individual accomplishment of intersection. There was apparent discontinuity between the various entry points into the ZPD and the later accomplishment.

Alternative frameworks, such as Piaget's, seek continuities between steps of independent development, an enterprise which has come under concerted attack in recent years. Fodor (1980) points out the problem with the Piagetian constructivist position that arises when one attempts to derive a formal mathematical model of stage development: a higher order calculus or logic can derive lower order ones but cannot be derived from them; hence, it is very difficult to see how children can progress from "lower" logical stages to "higher" logical stages unless one posits (as Fodor would) that the "higher" stage is in some way innately in place and that what looks like constructivist stage development is in fact just the gradual maturation and environmental triggering of innate mechanisms. From Fodor's vantage point, the claim is that the innate biogenetically constrained cognitive constructs account for the "highest" order logic (formal operational) and that earlier logics (sensorimotor, concrete operational) which can be derived from them appear under certain maturational and (minimal) environmental conditions. The argument as applied to Piagetian theory appears to be sound.

In the same article, Fodor develops a critique which he apparently believes reduces a Vygotskian position to an innatist theory.[2] But his analysis is incorrect; in fact, in an interesting way, Fodor's argument provides its own contradiction. He considers the "typical" concept learning experiment in which the subject is given a stack of cards of different colors and shapes and is asked to sort them into piles which might be labeled with a nonsense word such as "miv." The experimenter provides some materials, and some interactions and differences in these conditions are studied to see what conditions promote, say, faster learning. Fodor claims that such work can develop information on rate of learning and influences on learning ("fixation of belief") but cannot inform the investigator about where concepts come from, leaving inquiries about "concept acquisition" to the nativist.

But Fodor in fact tells us just where the concept comes from: *it comes from the experimenter.* There is a social origin for the concept, just as Vygotsky assumes. Of course in the case that Fodor uses ("miv" is red and square), the society which originates it is rather odd, small and restricted (the laboratory society) and the social interactions are rather dull and limited (the experimental procedure script), but nonetheless, the social origin is clear. It is even important in some such experiments that the concept being investigated comes only from this restricted little society, lest unknown variance from prior history vitiate the conclusions. (Where else could "miv" for instance, come from except from some society of experimental psychologists?)

---

[2] It is important to note that the sociohistorical school, and particularly Vygotsky, are not in principle opposed to positing innate elements; work in the framework includes work on biological materialism and phylogenetic inquiry. It is consistent with this framework to posit that some aspects of mind originate and are constrained biogenetically and that others originate and are constrained culturally. This is similar to a position Chomsky presented at the conference where Fodor developed his critiques (Piattelli-Palamarini, 1980).

Fodor is wrong with respect to Vygotsky's theory when he says, "What it doesn't tell you is where the hypotheses (and the concepts they deploy) come from!" (p. 146). Vygotsky claims and Fodor himself describes the experimenter as the most immediate origin of the experimental subject's concept. Fodor is correct, with respect to Vygotsky's theory, when he says "...it presupposes the availability of that concept" but is evidently unaware that the theory presupposes that the concept is available in the social system and that this is a reasonable alternative to Fodor's supposition that the concept must be presupposed available via a biological system.

More recently, Bereiter (1985) has addressed the Fodor paradox and similarly dismissed a Vygotskian approach:

Following Vygotsky,...one might formulate the following explanation: Learning does, indeed, depend on the prior existence of more complex structures, but these more complex cognitive structures are situated in the culture, not the child... Through...shared activities the child internalizes the cognitive structures needed to carry on independently. Such an explanation, satisfying as it may appear, does not eliminate the learning paradox at all. The whole paradox hides in the word "internalizes." How does internalization take place?

Bereiter speaks for many cognitive scientists in dismissing the sociohistorical school on the grounds that an adequate account of internalization is not found. Bereiter's article contains several very interesting points but also contains, in our view, several flaws which account for our different views of Vygotsky's theory and its usefulness as a means of understanding cognitive change. We discuss Bereiter's "theory of problematic learning" in more detail in the next section. In the present discussion of discontinuity and Fodor's paradox, we will point out one critical assumption that underlies Bereiter's argument.

Like many cognitive scientists, Bereiter assumes that the individual is the basic unit of analysis for the constructive processes by which new knowledge arises. In contrast to the prevailing view, we would propose that the constructive work occurs as much in the interaction between the adult and child as in the child's internal processes. The concepts of the zone of proximal development and appropriation already outlined in this chapter provide a framework for an answer to Bereiter's question about how internalization of more complex structures takes place. In a ZPD, processes of appropriation operate

externally to construct complex structures without depending on continuity with whatever simpler structures may have been useful for the
child's initial entry into the zone. Furthermore, in a ZPD, processes
of appropriation operate to revise the initial constructions of individual children. Because the construction is external, children do not
have to do the building of more complex structures by themselves.

Internalization, by definition, is an individual process. It is also a
constructive process rather than an automatic reflection of the external events. But the child does not have to leave the zone and then
work on internalizing in splendid isolation. The internal and external
constructive processes are occurring simultaneously. New, more
powerful structures may be constructed interpsychologically and the
new structure can interact with the child's intrapsychological structures to result in individual cognitive changes. This process of internalization is not at all automatic or unproblematic. But neither is it
logically impossible. Individual internalization is not the only locus of
constructive processes and therefore does not have to bear the whole
burden of a constructivist theory. This is not to say that we have mag-
ically solved the problem of development. We are suggesting that
Bereiter's dismissal of the Vygotskian position is premature. Internalization need not be the constructive process which creates the
more powerful structures. We are pointing to the social interactions
in the zone of proximal development as the more central locus for
constructive activity in the Vygotskian framework.

The logical paradox is one only for theorists who have some independent reason to believe that cognitive change is continuous with a
child's prior simpler system. A sociohistorical theory emphasizes the
productive intrusion of other people and cultural tools in the process
of cognitive change.[3] The undefended assumption of the primacy of
the individual makes it difficult for cognitive scientists to see how it is
that "internalization" and "more from less complex" cease to be a
difficulty for the sociohistorical school. Since it is individuals who are
changed, most cognitive scientists take it for granted that the search
for the processes of change need not look beyond the individual. That

---

[3] Examples of external instrumentality for development are given throughout the
book. More detailed answers about internalization can be found in the studies of
memory, language, arithmetic, and problem-solving found, e.g., in Vygotsky (1987),
Luria (1932, 1978), Davydov (1975), Istomina (1975), and Markova (1979).

this is not a logically necessary position can be seen most clearly by reflecting on the unhappy consequences of transporting the assumption to another domain – biological birth. One could not say "Since it is individuals who are reproduced, the search for the processes of reproduction need not look beyond the individual." Bereiter places the child alone on the cognitive construction crew; other people and the history embedded in cultural tools can only be resources. Every case we consider in this book involves joint construction of cognitive change. Questions about how the child gathers and makes use of resources that appear unanswerable in the individual framework are rendered moot in a framework that does not labor under this assumption. In their place are answerable questions, about how the construction team, including the child, coordinates the work in the zone. By directly examining the "construction zone," we can rediscover the continuity of change which is lost when children are examined in isolation.

The units in a theory of cognitive change

Bereiter's (1985) discussion of Fodor's paradox also illustrates a tendency among psychologists to divide domains of study in an *a priori* and mechanistic manner, making theoretical integration all the more difficult. Our major disagreement with Bereiter has to do with the atheoretical, descriptive approach he chooses to take. In its place we want to suggest that cognitive change can be studied as change in "functional systems" (Luria, 1932) which are an integrative unit of analysis (Zinchenko, 1985) in that they cut across cognitive systems kept separate in Bereiter's approach.

There are many points on which we agree with Bereiter and other investigators of learning and development. For example, the heuristics for investigating the phenomena that he calls "problematic learning" can apply very well to our endeavor. We agree that there is a kind of "bootstrapping" process that makes it possible for children to acquire cognitive structures that are more complex than they start with innately. We also agree that bootstrapping may not be easily reducible to simpler processes and, in particular, that the simple processes humans share with computers are not the best candidates for explaining how it may happen. We agree that, although humans do have a rich innate endowment, investigating domains where development is chancy (i.e., not innately determined) provides a good arena for studying cognitive change. And, as the studies in this book attest, we agree with Bereiter's claim that the study of instruction will play a key role in cutting the Gordian knot of Fodor's paradox.

When Bereiter turns to listing the "resources" that the learner has available for the kind of bootstrapping necessary to solve cases of "problematic learning," we continue to find broad areas of agreement. For example, he talks about "piggy-backing...[that] makes use of mechanisms that evolved for other purposes," imitation, learning support systems. Many of these bear a strong resemblance to the basic themes of this book; they seem to be consistent with the socio-historical school. When he goes on to describe the concrete behavior settings in which these resources are deployed, and to claim that "behavior settings can come to exist internally," then, the complementarity of Bereiter's position and ours is even more striking. Why, then, does Bereiter's article end with a section entitled "Needed: A Science of Problematic Learning"? We believe that the sociocultural theory is just the framework he needs to help understand cognitive change and to give some coherence to his lists of heuristics, resources and strategies.

There is a substantial reason for concern about undertaking Bereiter's program of research without the guidance of a theoretical framework. The *a priori* distinctions he proposes as a starting point are not theoretically precise and, combined with the assumption of individual responsibility for knowledge construction, lead to unwanted implications about children who fail. Bereiter's strategy is to divide the field of learning and development into three parts and focus on only one. He wants to ignore learning (where change involves "the standard tactics of feedback, reinforcement [etc.]"), as well as development (where change is "...a matter of maturation of innate structures"), and focus instead on problematic learning (where change "must be built up through the resources for constructivity discussed in [his] paper"). These distinctions are somewhat vague as Bereiter, himself, admits: "It is not obvious, for instance, whether learning to read should be considered problematic according to this definition, although it is certainly chancy for some children" (p. 221). In fact, several items on Bereiter's list of "resources" show the need to consider the functional relations among the members of his triad: his "spare mental capacity" resource pulls simple learning in, his "piggy-backing" and "chance plus selection" resource pulls in biologically innate and developing systems. Elsewhere we have argued against similar compartmentalizing of learning into "level 1" and "level 2" because teaching approaches derived from such a theory contribute to making cognitive change "chancy" for significant numbers of children (Cole & Griffin (Eds.), 1987; Griffin & Cole, 1987). Here, we will simply reestablish our notion that cognitive change as a unitary phenomenon is a worthwhile starting place. Compartmentalization in psychology is not new and we would want to avoid returning to the "descriptive mosaical stage [that] proved ruinous for psychology," as Luria (1932:15) put it.

When we approach a situation of cognitive change, we view the activity in the ZPD as constituting a "functional system," a term from Anokhin (1969) characterized by Luria in the following way:

The presence of an invariant task, performed by variable mechanisms, which bring the process to a constant invariant conclusion, is one of the basic features distinguishing the work of every "functional system." The second distinguishing feature is the complex composition of the functional system. . . . (1979:124)

Luria used the functional system of respiration as an example to differentiate this from the notion of function of a particular tissue. He found functional systems an important construct for developing the field of neuropsychology. Following damage to one part of a patient's brain, he found that it was often possible for another part of the brain to take over the function. A functional system may also include a prosthetic device. The mechanism changes but the functional system remains intact.

The *interpersonal system* in the ZPD also constitutes a functional system in the same sense used by Luria. In Chapter 3 we introduced the notion of a "whole task," which is the task considered as a social system thus including the origin of the task. When we add to this the various technologies (written language, movie star cards, worksheets and so on) which are part of the activity, we see the functional system. The zone of proximal development is a fundamental functional system for cognitive change. In the case of activity within a ZPD, an invariant task may occur many times, but how the functional system is constituted may change. The work we report in this book was to see how these tasks got instituted in lessons and experiments, how they became tasks for the child, what the variable mechanisms were that constitute them, and how it is that there is such trouble in reaching the conclusion for some children on some occasions. Like Luria's, our functional systems involve biological, culturally elaborated, and socially instantiated mechanisms in variable relations to the invariant tasks that we investigate. As experimenters, we can analyze specific aspects of the functional system in any particular investigation, yet the unit of analysis itself retains the critical components for change.

Changing representations

As we move toward a theoretical position in which people are parts of interpersonal, socially constituted functional systems, it becomes necessary to reassess the standard assumption about internal representations. In Chapter 3 we discussed a variety of forms that intersection can take. We provided two analyses for the behavioral display we were looking for. A choice between these representations was not critical to our claims. The point was that several analyses are often possible for a given set of actions. In the same set of examples, we also showed that the "schema" could mediate both individual and social problem-solving. It is not only difficult to decide on a particular representation. The location of the representation in the functional system cannot be decided *a priori*.

The standard assumption is that there is a well-specified internal representation for a cognitive structure that underlies an individual's behaviors observed in a task situation. And it is assumed that the cognitive structure uniquely underlies the behaviors. In contrast, the theoretical position we are proposing focuses on the changes within the functional system and the variable cognitive and interpersonal mechanisms that play a part in the system. We see four specific areas of contrast. First, in this standard framework, behavior that does not fit the model is accounted for as still somehow conforming to the same representation, but "missing a component" or "missing a stage in development" or "missing a step in execution." In our functional systems, there may be variable representations corresponding to the variable mechanisms that can still get the task done. Second, in the standard framework, external devices, like talk and charts and writing, bear an opaque and perhaps uninteresting relationship to internal structures. In our mediational framework, they are windows into the evolution and appearance of cognitive constructs. They are an essential part of the functional system that gives the actors as well as the analysts access to the changes occurring. Third, in the standard framework, representations are static; communicative comprehension requires an equivalence of representations. In our historical framework, representations are dynamic and communication proceeds with a series of "as if" relations where partial constructs are appropriated and revised. Fourth, in the standard framework, uniformity of representations makes it necessary to develop special constructs to handle the creative aspects of behavior. In our cultural framework, the inherent variation, which at times is recognizable as creativity, is subject to the social processes in which temporary alliances are created. We start with the assumption of inherent variation and see in the interpersonal processes the channeling and sometimes the destruction of the variations.

Once we attempt to integrate the internal and external processes and begin to consider the dialectic between the inter- and intrapsychological planes, the four standard assumptions are called into question. While abandoning these assumptions, cognitive science gets in exchange the richness of tools like "appropriation" and the flexibility of being able to observe the external analogues of the "hidden" internal structures which we understand to be created among people and to be mediated by culturally elaborated systems like language or written symbols.

The direction of cognitive change

Using the functional system as the unit of analysis for studying cognitive change has an impact on where and what we see change headed toward. As a consequence of interactions in the ZPD, the child's entering organization of psychological functions will likely be modified. We expect that the child system will approximate the system of interactions constructed in the zone. As we pointed out in Chapter 3, these will be dominated by the *adult* (expert) system of understandings with respect to the activity at hand. The asymmetry in the social relations that hold between an adult/expert and a child/novice provide the nonrelativistic directionality of change within and from the ZPD exchanges.

In other approaches to cognitive change, directionality comes from the domain: "the truth" of mathematics, geography, etc., is the endpoint toward which systems of learning and development are pointed. In this approach, directionality is organized by cultural historical factors.[4] If the child subsequently performs the task in a new situation, the new system functions displayed by the child are seen as the "next step" of the *intra*psychological system, attributable now to the child and available for the child as he coordinates in new interpsychological situations with teachers or peers or in the relative isolation that we would call "independent."

Placing the source of cognitive change in the social world should not imply that the child simply obtains a copy of the culture's knowledge through a process of direct transmission. Similar to Piaget's theory, the sociohistorical theory sees a process of construction at work. However, unlike Piaget's approach, Vygotsky emphasized the origins of knowledge in the social interactions the child engages in. This makes his theory interesting for us because it gives an important role to the teacher and helps to account for the variability in the process and its outcomes.

The variability of outcomes is the key to the creativity of the interactive system. Just as children find the goal of the task by engaging in the interaction (as we showed in Chapter 3), the teachers also discover possible goals for the episode or in addition to the specific lesson "objectives." The children may take the ZPD in unanticipated directions based on their own appropriation of what the teacher makes available. In this respect, the functional system of the ZPD may not be characterized by an invariant task – the task as negotiated by the teacher and child may in fact change. While the dominant task

[4] Aside from importance with respect to microgenetic and ontogenetic analysis, there is an advantage in this position for those attempting to account for the possibility of new inventions in domains like mathematics, geography, etc. If what can be learned or known is seen as a function of the currently existing domain, rather than as a function of cultural historical factors, then one is faced with the problem of explaining how simpler structures in the domain can give rise to more complex later developments in the domain. This is yet another version of the paradox raised by Fodor.

definition is that of the teacher and the dominant movement is toward the adult system, each step is an interactive construction with a variety of possible outcomes.

The following chapters apply this framework to theoretical and practical issues of education.

5   Assessment versus teaching

When cognitive change is considered as much a social as an individual process, new questions arise about when and how to track or measure change. Changes in the individual can be assessed in terms of the changing functional system which is the interactive construction zone. But the close relationship between assessment and instruction will be different for teachers promoting change than for researchers simply measuring it. Teachers must be constantly determining when it is fruitful to intervene (Burton & Brown, 1982). When is it possible and when is it necessary to appropriate a child's acts in order to promote cognitive change? Researchers conducting assessments are seldom required or able to make these *on-line* decisions.

A central resource for the teachers' decision making is the broad time frame that brackets their actions. On the one hand teachers know where the children have been: cumulative records indicate the skills the children acquired in the previous grades. Teachers often use a start-of-the-year test to form groups for purposes of instruction. The teacher we worked with did this, but she was not rigidly bound by the test results; she moved children around according to what she "knew" their real skills to be. Her teaching was also *prospective*. She knew the curriculum that was awaiting the children. In her sequencing of instruction she was mindful of the more complex problems they would encounter later on in the lesson, in the day, in the school year, and even later when they left her charge and were in the fifth grade.

In this chapter we reexamine the relationship between assessment and instruction in a set of interactions that highlight the importance of the prospective side of the teacher's time frame. The lesson we examine provides a case of the instructional interactions in which the procedures being taught will be directly instrumental in the next day's

76

lessons as well as crucial to the next phase of the same lesson. This immediate prospective constraint is reflected clearly in the teacher's structuring of the lesson. The case illustrates the tension between teaching and assessment and constrasts the work of the teacher and researcher.

Assessment by teaching: dynamic assessment

Assessment *while* teaching represents only one way in which assessment enters into the overall process of education. Perhaps the most familiar kind of assessment used in education is the standardized test. The teacher in our project used this kind of test at the beginning of the school year to assess the children's entering arithmetic skills and as a partial basis for forming the math ability groups. These techniques did not play a major role in our work and we will not examine them further here.

Another kind of assessment technique called "dynamic assessment" derives from a particular interpretation of Vygotsky's zone of proximal development (ZPD). When interpreted in the framework of psychological testing, the ZPD provides a very interesting alternative to the traditional standardized test. We used this "assessment by teaching" technique extensively in our cycles in the one-to-one tutorials which preceded and followed the group activities.

The concept of the ZPD contrasts strongly with what we might call a traditional view of learning in which the child moves through a sequence of increasingly difficult tasks or "learning hierarchy" (Gagne, 1968). The two conceptions lead to very different approaches to monitoring the child's progress and assessing his or her abilities. In the traditional view, competence is measured by successful performance of a task at a particular point in the sequence. Change over time is seen in improved performance of the task or in movement up the sequence. In either case, the child's individual performance is assessed. The ZPD provides a strikingly different approach (Feuerstein, 1979; Brown & Ferrara, 1985). Instead of giving the children a task and measuring how well they do or how badly they fail, one can give the children the task and observe how much and what kind of help they need in order to complete the task successfully. In this approach the child is not assessed alone. Rather, the social system of the teacher and child is dynamically assessed to determine how far along it had progressed.

We can illustrate dynamic assessment by considering again the "tutorial" from the Household Chemicals cycle discussed in Chapter 3. We called the technique a tutorial because we were not only assessing which children could do the procedure; we were also teaching them to do it. A portion of the tutorial illustrates these two aspects of the technique.

The tutorial was about combinations. We used stacks of cards with different movie stars both to assess children's abilities to make combinations and to teach a procedure for finding all the possible pairs of stars.

The procedure involved systematically pairing each star with every other star. After the child makes all the pairs that he can from five stacks of cards without assistance, the tutor provides a series of hints. First, she asks the child to check to see if they are all there. The tutor waits to see if the child will come up with a procedure like the one we wanted to instill. If the child does not, then the tutor asks if he has all the pairs with the left-most star. This is a low level hint since it does not tell the child what to do. It just suggests where he might start his considerations. If this hint does not get the child to do the target procedure, then the tutor gets more specific and asks if he has the pair consisting of the left-most star and the one to its right. Then the tutor asks, "Can you continue checking?" Each time a hint is acted on, the child is asked to continue before going on to the next specific hint. At any point that the child is able to make the next move on his own, the tutor discontinues the hints or provides only the low level hint (e.g., if Shawn were the second star from the left and the child faltered after completing a check of all the pairs with the left-most star the tutor asks, "Do you have all the pairs with Shawn?").

In general, the strategy in this tutorial-assessment method was to build the level of hints up to the point where the child could play a part in the procedure and then to begin reducing them again until the child was carrying out the procedure on his own. In this way we were able to find out two things: first, how much help the child needed in order to perform the checking procedure we had in mind; and second, how quickly, once the procedure was being carried out interactively, the child could take over the task as a more independent achievement. These are two aspects of dynamic assessment. The first assesses the child's current state in relation to the zone available for acquiring the concept. The second assesses the child's "modifiability" or readiness to learn. In order to serve each of these purposes, the tutor has to be careful not to give more help than is needed. If too much help is given (for example, if the tutor were to continue to lead the child through each step of the procedure without checking to see if the child could do it with a lower level of hints), it would be impossible to tell whether the child could have done the task with less help. Dynamic assessment, then, shares a feature in common with the traditional testing method of assessment in that it requires putting the child "on her own." Support has to be removed until the child begins to falter. One difference between the two approaches lies in the fact that dynamic assessment achieves a finer-grained idea of the child's level of "independent ability."

We do not wish to ignore the critical question of how to determine what "levels" to use in such methods. In the tutorials that we conducted during the course of our research, for example, we invented sequences that were plausible ordinal scales of "amount of help" but we made no attempt to determine that our sequence was more effective than other possible sequences. Determining the variety of sequences that are available and the cognitive consequences of different sequences would require further empirical research (of the sort described in Chapter 6 for a different problem domain, in which the ZPD is used as a location for observations of cognitive systems in the process of construction). Determining the levels within, the routes toward, and even the endpoints of a particular zone raises important issues which set research on cognitive change off from assessment as a tool for measurement. Here, however, we turn to another contrast as we examine the relationship between this kind of dynamic assessment and the assessment that occurs as an integral part of more normal instructional interactions.

Assessment while teaching

Assessment while teaching, i.e., as an integral part of the instructional process, is a critical part of instructional interactions

(Shavelson & Stern, 1981; Clark & Peterson, 1986). Through the use of a stimulated recall interview procedure, for example, McNair (1978–79) showed that the largest number of the decision points in a teacher's interactive teaching are motivated by concerns about whether the pupils are learning the lesson material. But as Wallen (n.d.) shows in his survey of elementary-level methods texts, methods for interactive assessment are seldom treated explicitly in teacher training. Instead they are generally left to practical experience and apprenticeship.

Assessment while teaching differs in at least three ways from the usual practice of dynamic assessment. First, the adult's priorities are reversed. In dynamic assessment the goal of teaching is subordinated to the goal of determining the child's independent level of achievement. The teacher subordinates assessment to instruction. Second, the teacher rarely has the luxury of working one on one with students for extended periods. At best, in the small-group settings, she can sample the apparent match between the children's behavior and the behaviors she expects as a part of her conception of the task. Third, many instructional units do not decompose themselves into a neat sequence of levels to be mastered in an invariant sequence with a single correct route to mastery, In fact, appropriable child behaviors come in great variety, requiring flexible expertise on the teacher's part to weave them into a productive instructional interaction.

These complexities of the actual conditions of instruction when compared with the conditions of dynamic assessment produce severe constraints on researchers who seek objective ways to assess (1) the children's independent level of achievement in the actual conditions of classroom instruction and (2) the effectiveness of teachers in promoting cognitive change. They render problematic, for example, our ability to address the implications of the fact that teachers must subordinate assessment to instruction or the closely related fact that the teacher's current teaching–assessment practices occur under the constraints of future tasks she knows the children will face.

Recognizing these complexities, we sought conditions within the instructional interactions created by our curriculum cycles where the structure of the task afforded a decomposition akin to that which obtains in the typical dynamic assessment situation but where the normal constraints of instruction still obtained. We encountered one such situation in the Household Chemicals cycle.

At a particular point in the cycle, children were posed two variants of the same task, one right after the other. We reasoned that it would be possible to assess the amount of support that the teacher provided in the children's first encounter with the task and then compare it with the amount of support that she provided on the second encounter. *Decrements in the amount of support would indicate an increase in the children's independent ability to carry out the task.* By specifying the amount of help the teacher gave, we felt we could obtain a snapshot of her assessment of the children's abilities.

The chemical indicator lesson

As part of the Household Chemicals cycle we developed a lesson sequence that would give the children hands-on practice with mixing chemicals and recording results on a worksheet. These skills were taught in part in order to teach methods of scientific thinking. They were also skills that would be needed for the chemical combinations activities described in detail in Chapter 3.

The teacher taught the lessons to five groups of four to six children. Each group spent 25 minutes in a lesson where, for the first time, they actually got to mix chemicals. The lesson had three main phases. First, the teacher discussed the classification of chemicals and the use of indicators to identify them. The children were told how iodine turns starch purple and how red cabbage solution changes to different colors when mixed with an acid or a base. Then, the teacher had the children pair up and distributed two chemicals and the two indicators to each pair. Each pair was to mix each of their chemicals with each of their indicators and record the four reactions on a worksheet. Although the teacher told pairs of children to work together, each individual was, in effect, given responsibility for only one chemical. All that any one child had to do was mix his or her chemical with each of the two indicators and record the results of each mixture. In a final phase of the lesson, the teacher planned to discuss the results with the group of children and review what could be said about each chemical as an acid, a base, or a starch. Since each pair of children was to obtain 4 results, she anticipated a discussion in which 8 to 12 chemical-indicator results would have to be collated for the systematic comparisons that would allow them to appreciate the basic distinctions upon which the lessons were based. As it turned out, the hands-on activity ran overtime for all the groups and it was decided to have a separate large-group lesson in the afternoon to discuss the results.

The consequence of these plans and procedures was that at the time the children began testing chemicals and indicators, the goals of the teacher and children were systematically different. The teacher's goal was to prepare the children for the later parts of the lesson sequence, in particular, phase 3 of the planned lesson and more distantly, the chemical combinations tasks.

The children knew nothing of this future. They were being allowed to mix chemicals for the first time! While their goals cannot be specified *a priori*, they could not have included the future that was planned for them. From their talk and their actions, it seems safe to say that at least one of their goals was to "see what happened."

Changes in amount of help

Focusing on the actual sequence of testing their chemicals with each of two indicators, we felt safe in claiming that if children need less help to get a problem done the second time they do it, then we, and the teacher, could conclude that they had learned something. We coded the lessons with respect to whether or not the children received help from the teacher at various points in the mixing and recording part of the lesson. We started our coding after the teacher's initial instructions just as she distributed the chemicals. At the most macro level we were concerned with differences between the first and second task, that is, between the child's mixing the chemical with the first indicator (and then recording the results) and mixing the chemical with the second indicator (and recording). We expected that the kinds of problems encountered with respect to choosing the two chemicals and mixing them in the test tube would be quite different from the problems encountered in recording the chemicals and results on the worksheet. So within the first and second task we coded the Mix and Record phases separately.

We also wanted to code the usefulness or importance of the help because it was intuitively clear that some of the help the teacher gave was somehow more significant than other help. This difference proved very difficult to code, however, and we were unable to attain reliability on our initial attempts. The utility of help is, of course, an interaction between what the teacher says and what the child already knows. For example, explicit detailed instructions constitute a high-level utility only for a child who does not know what to do.

Our first, partially successful, solution to the "utility" problem keyed off a distinction the teacher, herself, made when we interviewed her about the help she was giving. She distinguished between "low-level" and "high-level" help – by which she was referring to telling them simply that they should do the operation or explaining how actually to do it. We labeled these two aspects of each operation "Step" and "Execute." As it turns out, the patterns of results are quite different for these two aspects of teacher help.

For each child there were eight points to be coded as to whether or not the teacher provided help (two indicators by two operations by two aspects). Two coders assessed the reliability of this procedure by coding one of the lessons independently. They agreed on 91% of the cases.

Figure 5.1 shows the results for each of the eight coding points. For the moment, consider the whole bars indicating the total amount of help provided by the teacher, ignoring the fact that there are gray areas on each bar. The patterns for Mixing and Recording are quite different. For Mixing there is a decrease in the amount of help from the first to the second combination with respect to the Execute aspect but not for the Mix aspect. This decrease in help for the execution of Mixing is found separately in each of the five small groups. The children continued to get the same help throughout the lesson on the Step aspect.

The results for the Recording operation of the tasks are quite different. Here there is no difference in total help between the first and second task. The teacher help stays at a relatively constant high level throughout the lesson. The results suggest that the children were learning something about how to do the mixing over the course of the lesson but that they did not learn anything about how to record the results. But another interpretation is just as plausible. It could be that the children did learn but that the teacher went ahead and told them

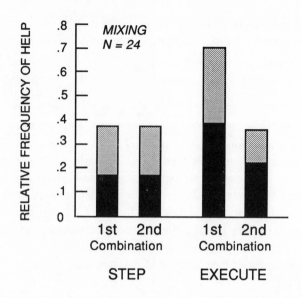

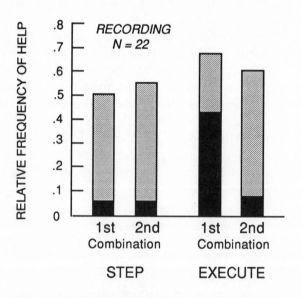

Figure 5.1. Relative frequency of teacher help for each of eight coding points. "Grey areas" of each bar indicate help that could not be determined by the coder to be needed.

what to do anyway. The resolution of the problem requires us to re-examine the issue of what it means for a teacher to help a student.

Was the help needed?

The possibility that the teacher provided "unneeded" help forces us back to consider the interactive nature of the help. Once we coded whether or not the teacher gave help (and what operation and aspect it was given in), we returned to considering whether or not the children appeared to need the help the teacher gave. We applied three coding categories to each of the eight coding points. Reliability of two coders working independently was 87%. The categories were:

1. Needed help. We had no trouble identifying many cases of the first category where children needed help. Children often asked for help in a question directed to the teacher or they sat doing nothing until the teacher told them what to do.

2. Did not need help. We also identified many cases where the children did not need help to complete the procedure successfully and, in fact, got no help. There were, however, a few cases where children got help but clearly did not need it, e.g., they were already doing the step when the teacher told them to do it.

3. Cannot tell whether help was needed or not. The third coding category was more problematic but points to an important difficulty with assessing children's abilities within instructional interaction even in the slightly rarified context of this lesson. There were a large number of cases where we could not tell whether or not the children needed the help they were given. These were not cases of inadequate data collection; the teacher–child interactions were recorded clearly enough. Rather they were cases where the teacher gave help *before* it was clearly needed. For example, many of these cases were ones in which the children asked the teacher about how to describe the color of the resulting reaction. The teacher would answer that question and immediately go on to tell them to write it down. As researchers, we could not determine if the children would have recorded the reaction on their own if they had not been given help.

The gray areas in each of the bars in Figure 5.1 indicate those cases for which we could not tell if the help was needed. This figure makes it clear that the interventions directed toward the problem of mixing the chemicals were relatively more responsive to the children's problems or questions than the interventions around recording. A closer look at the Mixing data indicates that, excluding the gray areas, we have the same pattern of results as we found when those areas were included. That is, the Step aspect shows no change but there is a decrement in the help with the second combinations for the Execution aspect.

Looking now at the Recording data we find quite a different pattern when we exclude the gray areas. Here a far greater proportion of the teacher's interventions did not follow a child's question or problem. While the Step aspect stays the same from the first to the second combination, the Execute aspect shows a *decrease* in the amount of help that we can be sure was needed. That is, we do find a decrease in the difficulties and questions the children had, but the teacher continued to give a high level of help.

Teaching and assessment in conflict

In terms of the ordinary concept of dynamic assessment taken from one-on-one situations, the teacher seemed to be obscuring our view of the children's competence. The decrease in requests for help suggests that the children *were learning something about recording results* on their worksheets. But other interpretations are also plausible. For example, the teacher may have believed that the children did not know how to Execute recording so began giving help a little sooner the second time in order to head off the difficulty.

On the basis of further analysis and a consideration of the lesson sequence as a whole, we prefer a different interpretation which speaks directly to the difference between teaching in order to assess and assessment as a part of normal instruction. The teacher also coded some of the lessons and discussed with us her perceptions of her interventions. These interviews provided us with several plausible explanations for the differences in the patterns of teacher help for

Mixing and Recording. First, she pointed out that she actually provided specific instructions about mixing in the first phase of the lesson but gave far less explanation about using the record sheet in that phase. Thus the greater level of help for recording may be partially a result of attempting to provide mini-lessons on recording during the "hands-on" phase. Second, the teacher felt she had to make extra effort to assure the records were kept because of the next phase of the lesson she was preparing the children to undertake. If the children did not know what to do next as far as mixing is concerned, they would be stuck and would stop or ask a question. But it would be very easy for a child to mix a chemical and indicators, examine the result, replace the test tube in the rack, and then go on to the next combination without recording the results. This would be an easy mistake for the children to make because the purpose of the record could be found only in the third phase of the lesson in which the 12 chemical combinations were to be discussed and which only the teacher knew about. She noted that many of the interventions that we had coded as category 3 (cannot tell) were cases in which she considered herself to be just reinforcing the actions she presumed the child would probably carry out anyway. But she knew that subsequent lessons in the unit (e.g., the chemicals combination task) would make use of the same record-keeping skills and she wanted to use whatever opportunities she had to reinforce the record-keeping habit.

The teacher's comments point to an important way in which teaching and assessment can be in conflict. *Giving too much help is usually not a critical problem for teaching.* If the children get help with a problem when they do not need it, the worst that can happen is that they will become a little bored and perhaps want to get onto something new or into something inappropriate. A teacher can afford to err in the direction of giving too much help, but the consequences may be far more disturbing if too little help is given. Dynamic assessment of the children's progress in being able to solve a problem requires withdrawing support to the edge of the children's abilities. This kind of brinksmanship requires that the teacher be there to quickly pick the children up when they do slip over the edge of their competence.

Some forms of teacher–child instructional interaction avoid this problem. For example, where teacher–child interaction is a series of questions to the child (cf. Mehan, 1979; Griffin & Humphrey, 1978), the discourse provides a structure for fine-grained assessment. Questions can be used to present a small task for the child or for the group of children being taught. If the children fail to answer adequately, the teacher can reframe the question, thus providing more help. The questioning style of interaction, thus, in a limited way can avoid the problem of giving too much help.

These results point to a principled limitation on analysts' abilities to achieve their goal of coding teacher effectiveness and student achievement. The "gray area" indicating a zone of ambiguity is not an "error of analysis." Rather, it points to the *inherent ambiguity* present when the constraints on the teacher's goals go beyond the immediate context to include future goals of which the present lesson is a part. This important fact about instructional interaction corresponds to the difference between a view of instruction as the construction of zones of proximal development and assessment as a measure of children's distance from a preset goal to be achieved in the context at hand.

Using dynamic assessment as a model for "assessing while teaching" has important limitations beyond the "gray areas" we found in the present analysis. The assumption of a fixed endpoint or "closed future" is considered essential to the quantification of student levels required for assessment (Brown & French, 1979; Campione, Brown, Ferrara & Bryant, 1984). In contrast, the ZPD points to a way of observing and describing the process of change, not simply measuring the change against a preconceived standard. As Campione et al. recognize, the ZPD concept is more correctly characterized by looking for where a student can go with a little help than with quantifying the amount of help needed to reach a standard endpoint. In Chapter 6 we analyze the interpsychological activities involved in the construction of the division procedure. In that case the different routes the children took through the zone and where they ended up at the end of the lesson are themselves treated as empirical issues. Hence, by attending to the observable constructive activity carried out by the teacher and the children, we can begin to sort out the different constructs which different children are working with even though all begin with a task that is articulated at the start as standard for all. These kinds of observations form the empirical basis for a theory of cognitive change. In many ways, the teacher is more like a cognitive researcher than a tester. Teaching a variety of children involves a qualitative tracking where the route and endpoint are not clearly known in advance. In the course of a lesson, adjustments are more often qualitative than quantitative. The constraints on the teacher's cognitive research are enormous, as we have seen in this chapter, but the general principle of assessment in relation to, and in the course of, ongoing instruction provides a useful understanding of a teacher's work.

6   Social mediation goes into cognitive change

(with Andrea Petitto)

In this chapter we use an analysis of a fourth-grade lesson on the division algorithm to demonstrate that the transmission of procedural skills can be observed in interactions that take place in the zone of proximal development. However, that transmission cannot be reduced to direct instruction of procedures. Teacher–child interaction includes a process of appropriation in which the critical aspect of the division task emerges. The chapter illustrates the interactive construction of cognition, showing the inseparability of social and cognitive processes.

The division cycle proved an exceptionally good example of the dynamics of cognitive change for our purposes. Although division instruction appears at first to require only transmission of a very straightforward algorithm, it turns out to be not quite so simple to teach (Petitto, 1985). The problem facing the student can be phrased as follows: the student must acquire the concept, "gazinta" (goes into). At the outset, the child is confronted with the confusing request to say how many times "5 gazinta 27." Before this time in the arithmetic curriculum, the child has worked on "number facts," viz., "five 5s are 25; five 6s are 30" and only "three 9s" or nine 3s" are 27. So, how can 5 "go into" 27? Five can "go into" 25 or 30; but only 3 or 9 can "go into" 27! Expert skill in carrying out the procedure actually calls for an initial estimate of the quotient, which is then checked and adjusted in the subsequent steps. Without getting into the details at the outset, suffice it to say that the initial step of estimating is a very difficult thing to explain to the novice who does not yet know what it is that one is attempting to estimate! In other words, the goal of estimating the quotient and the procedure of successively approximating it must somehow be taught simultaneously. This process requires what

90

is often referred to as "bootstrapping" by cognitive psychologists. The bootstrapping that this situation calls for makes direct instruction difficult or perhaps impossible, yet generations of fourth graders who have mastered the procedure can attest that the problem is not insurmountable. If direct instruction is acknowledged as impossible, some alternative process must be found. The alternative that we discovered is the process of appropriation and interpsychological construction. This set of lessons on division provides an excellent illustration of how appropriation and construction work (and how they sometimes do not work).

Division was also a good example of cognitive change in instruction because the division cycle in which it was embedded was planned and implemented differently from the other cycles. In all but one of the units that we and the teacher implemented, there was a tracer task defined in terms of a laboratory task with which we, as researchers, were familiar. In the division cycle one of the teachers designed the unit herself. Instead of a set of differently organized activities all instantiating the same task, this unit consisted of a sequence of lessons each taught to five math-ability groups. Consequently the same task (in this case, the teacher's lessons on division) was carried out under five very different conditions defined by the ability levels of the groups instead of several isomorphs applied to the same children. The algorithm was well known and was not difficult to specify as a set of goals and subgoals even though it was and remains a difficult problem to transmit it to fourth graders. Consequently, the division cycle provided us a natural experiment that allowed us to observe how the teacher's task was carried out or subverted under the different interactional conditions presented by the ability groups using the concept "division" as a tracer.

Direct instruction versus spontaneous invention

We can express the central theoretical point of this chapter in terms of what seems to us to be a false dichotomy. In psychological research on cognitive change and instruction there is a tendency to distinguish between the external stimulus consisting of what the teacher says and the internal process by which the organism incorporates these external events into existing mental structures. For example, in Piaget's work we find a distinction between "cultural transmission" and "equilibration" (cf. Piaget, 1973). Transmission essentially involves the subject's accommodation to the specific beliefs and mores of the culture. Equilibration refers to the process by which the subject's own actions come into balance with each other. Equilibration is a creative process of invention for Piaget, who goes farther than almost anybody in asserting the individual construction of general logical principles. In fact, he argues that direct instruction will actually inhibit the child's understandings if instruction gets in the way of the child's own exploration. Piaget's distinction turns into a dichotomy because he excludes any intermediate process. Cultural transmission becomes identified with a coercive social process of direct instruction. The possibility that there are cultural transmission processes that are (in part) not experienced coercively and that these processes require the child's active participation is not considered.

We find a similar tendency to dichotomize external and individual sources of cognitive change in more recent work in cognitive science which has developed detailed models of the process of skill acquisition by examining in-process transformations of individual problem-solving behavior (Anzai & Simon, 1979; Anderson, 1982; diSessa, 1982; Resnick, 1982). These researchers have long since abandoned the model of the passive learner, arguing that teaching cannot be construed as "telling," i.e., direct transmission of knowledge. This is particularly true in procedural learning. Anderson (1982), for example, points out that a major difficulty with the idea of direct procedural instruction is that it requires the specification of new productions that will be adequately integrated with the student's "complex existing flow of control." Resnick and Glaser (1976) have argued that learners must actively "fill in" gaps in instruction, making connections that are only implicit in the teacher's presentation. In this approach, as in Piaget's, the processes which produce individual learning are internal and inaccessible to direct observation. Investigation of such processes must infer the nature of those processes from their products – however fine-grained that sequence of products might be.

Our analysis of the actual process of instruction of the division algorithm illustrates the idea that there are processes which must properly be characterized as *interpsychological* – arising from the interaction between people – which play a major role in producing cognitive changes. These interactive processes are accessible to observation and can provide an important link to explain cognitive change.

The analysis presented below reveals several aspects of this process. First, in initiating the lesson, the teacher presents a precise procedural description which serves as a medium of interaction between herself and the children. In the process of the interaction, the form of the procedure which the students learn changes from the procedural description originally presented by the teacher to alternate but equally valid procedures, including successive approximation, among others. As will become clear in the analysis, these changes lead to final versions of the procedure that differ from student to student. Yet these variations are neither spontaneous inventions by the students nor are they planned in advance by the teacher. The procedures exist and can be seen as the interaction between teacher and child. Variations in the form of the student – teacher interaction are indistinguishable from variations in the form of the long division procedure. These variations follow certain characteristic patterns, some of which are associated with achievement levels of individual students.

Description of the division cycle

We will focus our attention on one lesson in the sequence of eight lessons that the teacher planned for getting the children to learn to divide. This sequence started with dividing up groups of manipulable blocks and ended with the "bring-down" algorithm. The year before we heard fourth graders chanting to themselves one notion of this algorithm, "divide, multiply, subtract, bring down." The lesson we analyze was a stumbling block for some of the children who did not progress to the final topic.

The entire sequence was part of a larger sequence of the elementary school arithmetic curriculum. Long division is prepared for in the earlier grades by subtraction and multiplication. The particular algorithm that was taught is not, of course, the only available method for efficiently doing division (a hand calculator is far more efficient) but it is the one that fifth-grade teachers will expect the children to know – in fifth grade they learn to do the same algorithm with two-digit divisors. By focusing on one of the lessons we do not want to lose sight of the fact that in planning the lesson, the choices that were available to the teacher were highly constrained by her knowledge of the children's prior preparation and by expectations about where they were going (see also Chapter 5 for the impact of time of teaching).

A critical skill that will be needed for long division with two-digit divisors is the process of successive approximation because the initial step of finding a likely candidate for the quotient cannot straightforwardly make use of commonly memorized multiplication facts. Estimation and successive approximation are seldom directly taught even though they are very useful for many kinds of everyday arithmetic (Lave, Murtaugh & de la Rocha, 1984). These processes are not precision operations as are, for example, multiplication and subtraction, which can be carried out mechanically. Estimations are inherently goal directed. As an implicit aspect of fourth-grade arithmetic, these processes are particularly interesting in the current context.

The children's preparation for division was, to some extent, encoded in the ability groups into which the class was divided. We begin this outline of the division lessons with an account of the ability grouping. Then we show in global terms how these groupings apparently interacted with the plan for the sequence of lessons. We then turn to an analysis of the pivotal lesson and the process of emergence which it displays.

The math-ability groups

Educators have long had to struggle with the problem of organizing effective instructions for a heterogeneous student population. In classroom practice in the United States, this problem has most often lead to ability grouping – dividing students into small working groups according to a teacher's perception of the students' academic abilities. Teachers use small-group instruction to promote more student–teacher interaction and to increase student attentiveness during lessons (Barr, 1975). Children of similar academic ability are grouped together to facilitate the adjustment of teaching techniques to instructional needs. For pragmatic reasons such as these, the practice of ability grouping is well established.

For the purpose of arithmetic lessons, the teacher had divided her children into five small groups on the basis of tested arithmetic achievement in computation skills. These were routinely administered paper-and-pencil tests developed by project TORQUE (Education Development Center, 1979). They included two tests on number lines (one addition, one subtraction) and two multiplication tests. Although these test results formed the basis for assigning children to groups, the teacher did not strictly adhere to them. In a few cases she placed children into groups higher or lower than their arithmetic test scores would have indicated. The teacher justified these adjustments by noting that those who had been placed above their tested scores showed "systematic rule errors" in their written work, a fact which she interpreted to mean that their difficulties were not in "understanding" but were mechanical. The teacher felt that the two children whom she dropped to a lower placement generally "didn't seem to understand things." The average arithmetic test scores for each group are summarized in Table 6.1. The resulting groups consisted of four to six children each. The *number* of groups formed was not determined by the distribution of test scores but by the teacher's organizational plans for the rest of the time in the classroom.

The plan for the division unit

Despite differences in skill levels, the teacher used the same basic lesson plan for all groups. She did not expect that the "same lesson" would turn out to be the same for each group, however. Rather, she expected to make on-line modifications in response to what the children did in each of the small-group sessions. Even if planning time were unlimited and it were possible to plan a different lesson for each ability group, too little is known about the microgenesis of long division for her or the researchers to be able to predict the precise strengths and limitations of the different groups. Note in Table 6.1 that in addition to creating ability groups that differed in average level of prior knowledge, the grouping procedure created groups of quite different degrees of heterogeneity. The standard deviations in the lower three groups are four times the standard deviations in the top two groups. Thus, even five different lesson plans, one for each group, may not have been enough, since the hetero-

Table 6.1. *Results of arithmetic pretests for the five achievement groups*

		Average score (max = 28)	Std. dev.	Number of children
Highest achievers	Group 1	26.8	0.75	6
	Group 2	25.6	0.89	5
	Group 3	22.8	4.1	6
	Group 4	14.2	4.9	6
	Group 5	15.8	3.8	4

Scores are the number correct of 6 addition, 8 subtraction and 14 multiplication problems. Averages shown here are from the final group compositions which are not strictly in line with arithmetic scores since the teacher also used other indicators based on her previous interactions with them.

geneity of the lower groups could motivate many plans within each group! In the face of all these complications, then, a single but modifiable plan for all the groups was a reasonable solution. Thus came about the lesson plan that guided the sequence of tasks presented to each of the groups.

Arithmetic the children already knew. Division was not an entirely new topic. What was really new in this sequence of lessons was the idea of remainders. Most of the children knew the multiplication facts up to 9×9 and those who had not memorized alll the facts were at least very familiar with the format $a \times b = ?$ Simple division had been introduced earlier in the year. These earlier lessons consisted of one-digit divisors with one- or two-digit dividends and resulted in a single-digit integer solutions with no remainder. Figure 6.1 provides an index to the terminology and form of the division procedures. Simple division was taught as "reverse multiplication" and was written using division brackets that play an important part in the more complex algorithms. There were two steps in the simple division procedure: finding the quotient, then checking it. Finding the quotient was treated as a simple lookup for the missing member of the multiplication triplet ($a \times b = c$, where either a or b is unknown). Checking the answer amounts to a justification in which a multipication is expressed in its usual com-

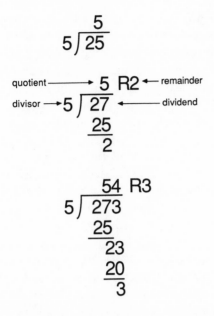

Figure 6.1. Simple division, simple division with remainders, and "bring-down" division.

plete form (*a* into *c* equals *b* because *a* times *b* equals *c*). In this form, simple divisions provided an alternative way of drilling multiplication facts.[1]

The sequence of lessons of division. There were eight lessons that covered six ways of doing division. Several of the activities were drawn from Souviney (1978), although the ordering of the methods did not strictly follow the usual manipulable-to-representational (analogical)-to-symbolic sequence. The teacher considered all the

---

[1] In this classroom, the usual method of practicing multiplication facts was to drill for speed and accuracy on randomly ordered multiplication triplets (*a* × *b* = ?). Thus, the children did not have a lot of practice with ordered sets of multiples (e.g., 7, 14, 21, 28, etc., as a sequence of answers for the 7 times table). Knowing the ordering of multiples is a skill that turns out to be useful for long division, as the teacher noted, in response to our discussion, and she reported that she would use that knowledge in planning future arithmetic lessons.

methods to be alternative ways to understand the idea of division with remainders. Only the last two methods, simple long division and long division with bring-downs, were considered to have a necessary ordering. The bring down method was the target procedure in that fourth graders are expected to learn it. In a sense, the other methods led up to this one by providing an array of alternative representations.

In the first lesson, a set of blocks was used to solve several division problems by sharing the blocks out among a number of groups or taking groups of a specified size out of the pile. Either method yields a quotient and a remainder. In the second lesson, children were introduced to the subtraction method in which the divisor is subtracted from the dividend and then subtracted again from the resulting difference and so on. In the third lesson, the children used Cuisinaire rods to solve problems similar to those in the blocks method but with larger numbers for which the "10-strips" came in handy. In the fourth lesson a pencil-and-paper version of the Cuisinaire rods was used. In the fifth lesson, which we focus on here, the children were introduced to simple long division with numbers and the "gazinta" sign. The sixth lesson was a review of all the methods for dividing and determining a remainder. The last two lessons introduced the bring down algorithm.

Group differences. All of the groups but one completed all the lessons. The lowest achievement group did not get beyond the lesson five topic of simple long division, so with this group the teacher returned to the lesson five topic after the lesson six review, rather than continuing on to the more complex algorithm. Analysis of the lessons indicated crucial differences in the process of the teacher–child interaction that accounts for the lack of further progress.

Introduction to simple division with remainders

Problems with two-digit dividends and a one-digit divisor were the focus of this lesson. Division is treated as a standardized procedure which generates a quotient, a number which is the multiple of the quotient and the divisor (and has no formal name in division), and a remainder which is the dividend minus the multiple. Constraints are that the remainder be positive and less than the dividend. All numbers are integers and from a restricted range, so that all problems would require and could be solved with simple division.

The lesson consisted of two clearly identifiable phases. It began with a demonstration and group participation sequence in which the teacher carried out several long division problems on the blackboard while individual children supplied portions of the solution. This was followed by a worksheet phase in which written work was done within the small-group session. In this phase, the children solved written problems individually, with the teacher providing help when she judged it beneficial.

In the demonstration, the teacher introduced long division as a variant of the simple division procedure followed by a new step to find a remainder. She first presented the long division problem, "7 into 46,"[2] to the group, then presented a closely related, "nearby" simple division, "7 into 42," writing both of them on the blackboard. She solved the simple division, then returned to the long division saying that it is done "the same way," by searching for a number which when multiplied by the divisor (7) would result in a multiple close to but smaller than the dividend (46): "What number times seven has an *answer* that's close to 46? . . . but it doesn't go over. If it's bigger than 46, then it won't work." At this point, after seeing the "nearby" simple division worked out, the children in all groups quickly filled in the correct quotient. The teacher then completed the problem by carrying out the multiplication as in the checking step ". . . because 6 times 7 is 42." She then demonstrated the subtraction step to find the remainder: "We subtract . . . this number [pointing to 42] from that number [pointing to 46] to find out what the difference is. . . . This is your remainder."

By indicating this relationship to simple divisions, the teacher has established a subgoal hierarchy for the long division procedure: first, find a nearby simple division; second, carry out the simple division; third, find the difference or remainder. Simple division is an already established routine consisting of two parts, reverse multiplication and check. Finding a remainder is a goal which has also been previously

---

[2] The teacher used different numerical examples in each group. The one presented for explanatory purposes here is from the second highest achievement group, but all others follow roughly the same course.

established through other instantiations of division with remainders using other media (manipulables of various types) and other procedures. But the goal of "finding a nearby simple division" is entirely new. (In the children's chant, it is the first element, "divide" that is new, while "multiply, subtract" are old and "bring down" is yet to come.) It is the divide step in the procedure that will be the focus of attention.

How can the students acquire goals they do not already have? Simply stating the goal of this step to students who are not already familiar with it would certainly be cryptic: e.g., "Find an approximate integer quotient less than the precise quotient but greater than any other integer quotient which is less than the precise quotient." Since statements such as this one would be uninterpretable by the average fourth grader (and perhaps the reader!), the teacher expressed the goal in terms of a procedure that would satisfy it. She re-solved the same problem, this time filling in the unspecified procedures with a sequence of precision operations.

The teacher's filled-in procedure begins by generating all the multiples of the divisor and scanning them for the one with the needed properties. In her presentation, she wrote out a list of multiples of the divisor on the blackboard, commenting that this step is normally done mentally: "So, that's what you would be doing in your head – trying to find all the answers that are *times*." Using this method, the teacher demonstrated the process of making proximity and relative magnitude judgments based on the sequence of multiples (35, 42, 49, etc.):[3] "Find an answer that's close to 46 but doesn't go over. Forty-nine is close but it goes over [pointing at the written list of multiples on the blackboard]. So 42 is the closest one that does... that isn't bigger." This completes the process of finding a nearby simple division.

Subsequently, the simple division is carried out in its original form, reverse multiplication and check: "What times 7 is 42? Six." The checking step follows all of the above procedures with the multiplication, "Six times 7 is 42," although this result had already been found within the procedures for finding the nearby simple division. The teacher completed the example by finding the remainder: "Sub-

---

[3] Rather than the sequence of multipliers (5, 6, 7, etc.).

tract and find your remainder. Remainder is 4. The answer is 6 remainder 4."

This is what we will call the *Extended Precision* version of the long division algorithm. The procedure as presented to each group sacrifices elegance for precision and completeness. No operations are unspecified, assuming that multiplication and subtraction do not require explanation. A child who remembers this sequence of steps in the proper order and who can execute each operation accurately is assured of success. Further, the Extended Precision sequence preserves intact the derivative relationship between long division and simple division.

However, the operations involved in identifying a nearby simple division put a great burden on memory by including steps which generate and search a long table of multiples. The checking step is redundant – repeating a result already obtained in earlier operations. These characteristics make it unlikely that an expert would actually use this method to do long division. Nevertheless, this form of the long division algorithm served as a medium through which the teacher and children negotiated new and more efficient procedures such as successive approximations.

As the teacher and children cooperated to solve the demonstration problems, and when they interacted in solving the worksheet problems, the actual procedures by which the problems were solved were changed from the Extended Precision version that the teacher originally presented. These transformations produced abbreviations and reorganizations, tending to shift the procedure from a tightly specified sequence of precision operations to more cognitively efficient processes which can include some elements of estimation.

Transformation of the procedure in interaction

Transformations followed two different routes drawing upon different aspects of the children's arithmetic skills. One route relied upon the children's knowledge of an ordered set of multiples of the divisor and produced an abbreviated version of the original algorithm in which the first two subgoals are merged. We will call this the *Precision Multiples* procedure. A second route relied on the children's ability to perform single multiplications but did not require familiarity with ordered sets of multiples. This second route led to the procedure we call *Successive Approximation*. It introduces an estimation strategy into the first two subgoals and recruits the remainder procedures to serve a checking function quite different from the original checking subgoal. As discussed above, this procedure itself implies the active existence of the long division goal which guides it. The following paragraphs present and analyze examples to illustrate the transformation processes.

Precision multiples

Of the two kinds of transformations observed, Precision Multiples represents a small but significant departure from the Extended Precision form. One example in which this transformation did involve an extended interaction sequence is presented here to demonstrate the interplay of elements in the interactive process.

Sometimes transformation processes took place within one problem and between one child and the teacher; sometimes a series of problems and several children were involved. The following example occurred over three problems solved in sequence by three different children, Jorge, Jenny and Tracy, interacting with the teacher during the demonstration phase in one small group session.

TEACHER: All right Jorge, your problem will be... [writes the division problem "9)49" on the blackboard]

JORGE: Forty-five. Five.

TEACHER: [writing 5 above the division brackets] Five times nine is...?

JORGE: Forty-five.

TEACHER: [writing 45 below the 49] OK, and then what?

JORGE: Four. Remainder four.

Jorge did not overtly carry out all the steps in the Extended Precision procedure, but he did report the results of each step; first the closest smaller multiple (45), then the corresponding multiplier (5). We cannot say whether Jorge mentally generated *all* the multiples of nine, though it is likely that he somehow abbreviated this part of the procedure. The teacher appropriated his answers to the Extended Precision form by writing in only the quotient, "5", and demanding the redundant multiplication step. Jorge complied (the second "45"), then finished by producing the results of the subtraction and labeled it the "remainder." Here, the overall form of teacher's original *sequence* of steps remained intact, though not all of the sequence is overtly carried out.

In two subsequent problems, this procedure was abbreviated and reorganized to eliminate the redundant multiplication. In the first of these, Jenny's answer was roughly the same form as Jorge's had been. The teacher then asked for further specification of the roles of these numbers in the algorithm sequence, this time by asking for their placement. Jenny's answer specified the placement not of the quotient but of the *multiple* – obviating the need for recalculating the multiplication. Thus, we see the first step toward eliminating the redundant multiplication.

[The teacher has written "7$\overline{)51}$" on the blackboard for Jenny to solve]
JENNY: It's 49. Seven times 7.
TEACHER: Here? Here? [pointing to positions above and below the division bracket]
JENNY: The 49 goes down under the 51. It's supposed to be 7. [The teacher writes in the 49 and 7 in their proper places]

In the third problem, Tracy began by specifying only the multiple and not the quotient (or multiplier) and specified its placement below the dividend. The teacher accepted this placement before any quotient was given. Only subsequently – and with a little difficulty – did Tracy determine the quotient.

[The teacher writes "8$\overline{)60}$" on the blackboard for Tracy to solve]
TRACY: Wait a minute. Fifty-six.
TEACHER: Here? [pointing above the division bracket]
TRACY: There, on the bottom. [The teacher writes in the 56] Um. Six.
TEACHER: Six times 8 is 56?
TRACY: [other children laugh] Wait. Seven! Seven. . .and four.
TEACHER: [writes in the seven and the four in their proper places] OK?

At this point, the Precision Multiples form of the procedure has emerged. The redundant checking step is merged with the procedures for finding a nearby simple division, and is completed *before* the quotient is completely determined.

The Extended Precision procedure called upon children's knowledge of multiplication of single-digit numbers. The children's adeptness at finding such multiples – once called upon to do so – allowed the teacher and students to modify sequences of operations into the Precision Multiples solution. The children demonstrated their readiness and the teacher was able to appropriate their responses into the lesson. The demonstration of readiness and the development of the new procedural sequence developed together. The old procedure, Extended Precision, served as a starting point and a medium of interaction between teacher and child. Through it, the teacher and children negotiated a new form of the procedure appropriate to the children's current arithmetic skills and level of understanding.

Successive approximations

In the above examples, the children drew upon knowledge of multiples of single-digit numbers to specify multiples of the single-digit divisors. Not all children effectively access knowledge of multiplication facts in this way, however. Some of the children showed a tendency to start with a likely quotient rather than a multiple. This tendency resulted in a different process of reorganization. The example below is from the same session as the preceding examples. Here, Thomas solves the problem "seven divided into 40" as follows:

THOMAS: Seven times four. Wait...That's not the closest. OK, it's supposed to be seven times five. Thirty-five...Four? Remainder four? Or, remainder, uh, five.
TEACHER: OK, you got that.

Thomas starts by stating a multiplication – multiplying the divisor by four. Then without overtly stating its result, he makes a judgment about its adequacy: "That's not the closest." Finally he adjusts, picking a larger *multiplier*. From his treatment of this multiplier, we must assume that it is intended to be the quotient although he never states this.

We cannot determine precisely what mental processes resulted in these verbal products. Thomas's problem solving is mainly internal and individual. Thomas's overt responses suggest a new process,

Successive Approximation, in which the first precision operation is the multiplication in the checking step which follows an estimation – finding an approximately correct quotient. However, similar transformations arose in extended teacher–child interactions which are more open to analysis. In one such case, Jackie had written "10 R 1" for the problem "nine into 84" on her worksheet.

JACKIE: Oh!
TEACHER: OK, so I think maybe you went too high.
JACKIE: Eight. What's 8 times 8? Eight times...72.
TEACHER: No. Oh, 8 times 9? Can you go higher than that?
JACKIE: Eight times 9 is 72? Just 9 times 9...Oh! [She erases and begins to redo the problem. The teacher turns her attention to someone else.]

When interacting with the teacher, Jackie clearly chooses multipliers without first deriving them from multiples of nine; note her hesitation after specifying the multiplication by eight. This characteristic of Jackie's approach interacts in complex ways with the teacher's instructional techniques and with the teacher's version of the long division algorithm. Jackie's multiplication was accurate and her multipliers were within a reasonable range, and so the teacher provided feedback on relative magnitude: "too high," "can you go higher?" The teacher's judgments are based on the relationship between 84 (the dividend) and multiples of nine (the divisor), consistent with the criteria for finding a nearby simple division. But Jackie acted on the higher/lower feedback by adjusting the *multipliers* of nine instead of the *multiples*. The net result is Successive Approximation, in which quotients are estimated and tried as multipliers of the divisor and subsequently checked.

Jackie's incorrect solutions are sufficiently reasonable to be interpreted in terms of the goal of finding a nearby simple division. The teacher's responses derive from a more tightly constrained version of that goal than is available to Jackie alone, though Jackie's and the teacher's goals overlap in their attention to magnitude relationships between multiples of the divisor and the dividend. Because of this overlap, the teacher needed only to express relational moves, providing external guidance which monitored relationships between the dividend and the outcomes of Jackie's actions. In this way, the goal itself is highlighted through the procedure to attain it. This procedure, however, is Successive Approximation, not the Extended Precision procedure.

In this and other examples observed throughout these sessions, a transformation to a Successive Approximation procedure began with a child's tendency to specify a quotient at the outset which, if not correct, was within a reasonable magnitude range. Errors by children using this approach led to correction efforts by either the child or the teacher which focused on relationships which specify the goal of the exercise.

These results illustrate that the form of the teacher–child interactions varies with different children and that these variations depend as much on the child's approach to the procedure as on the teacher's initial presentation and follow-up. The development of these interactional forms takes place through a complex interplay of factors involving division of labor on the task and mutual appropriation of responses and directives by the teacher and the children. These variations in the form of interactions are indistinguishable from variations in the form of the procedures which are the content of the lesson.

Resort to the initial presentation form

The Successive Approximation solution is an example of error resolution which occurred with relatively high-achieving children. As shown above, the errors that high achievers produced usually bore a sufficient resemblance to the correct answer to be interpretable, and so appropriable by the teacher, who could then choose a correction strategy. That is, the teacher could specify some parameter by which the child's solution procedure could be corrected: try a lower number, get closer, etc. With the lowest two groups, however, children who did not produce correct answers either remained silent or gave answers that were not readily interpretable in terms of the goal structure of long division. When this happened, the teacher resorted to the original form of the presentation of the algorithm, guiding the child through it step by step. The following examples illustrate this process.

In the second to lowest achievement group, three of the five children whom the teacher called upon were able to provide precise numerical solutions with little or no discussion. Two other children had some difficulty. Joel's attempt illustrates the form that the teacher–child interaction took when the child provides no initial input. [The teacher writes "7)͞5͞1" on the blackboard for Joel to solve. Joel is silent for some time. Others occasionally mutter that they know how to do it.]

TEACHER: Seven times what has an answer that's close to 51? [no response] Try a number. How about 7 times 3?
JOEL: No.
TEACHER: Seven times four?
JOEL: No.
TEACHER: Seven times five?
JOEL: No.
TEACHER: What's seven times six?
JOEL: No.
TEACHER: OK, how about seven times seven?
JOEL: Yes.
TEACHER: . . . or seven times eight?
JOEL: Yes.
TEACHER: Which one do you think it should be?
JOEL: Seven times eight.
TEACHER: OK, what's seven times eight?
JOEL: Fifty-six.
TEACHER: Fifty-six. Is that too big?
JOEL: Yes. Forty-nine. Seven times seven.
TEACHER: Good. Seven times seven is what again?
JOEL: Forty-nine.

Here, Joel's yes–no judgments and his numerical responses indicate that his multiplication is adequate to carry out the steps of the procedure once the teacher specifies them, but he contributes almost nothing that is not asked for. Though the teacher began by using terms which suggest an estimation strategy, "Try a number," the interaction results in the complete Extended Precision procedure close to its original form. Joel's yes–no responses to the teacher's "How about. . ." questions show that he does have some grasp of the criterial relationships between the multiples and the dividend, but he failed to establish this as an area of agreement between himself and the teacher at the outset.

This performance may have affected other children in the group.

The next child, Candy, began the division "four into 30" by stating the multiplication "four times two equals eight," apparently initiating the full form of the Extended Precision procedure. The teacher then followed along by helping her through the entire sequence of multiples of four.

The low-achieving children sometimes made initial responses that were not easy to interpret. In the lowest achievement group, during the worksheet phase of the session, Eric had made some calculation errors and an error in the placement of the results of his calculations. Because of these errors, he had written "16 remainder one" as a solution to the problem "three into 17"

TEACHER: What number times three is 16?
ERIC: Hmmmmmmmmm.
TEACHER: I think you'd better think about this one again. [The teacher erases the 16.] Think of your three's tables. What number times three has an answer that's close to 17?
ERIC: [No answer.]
TEACHER: Let's go for our multiplication tables. Three times one?
ERIC: Three. [said with a sigh]

Eric and the teacher then proceed through the entire multiplication table to complete the Extended Precision form of the algorithm.

Group differences in interaction

Our analysis of the teacher–child interactions showed that there were important differences in the *form* of these interactions across groups. These differences are displayed in Table 6.2. The Precision Multiples solution was observed in all ability groups, though not for all individuals in any one group. The Successive Approximations solution was observed *only* in the three groups highest in arithmetic achievement. Finally, the Extended Precision form of the long division algorithm as it was originally presented often reappeared in the teacher–child interactions in the lowest achievement groups, but very rarely in the highest ones.

In all groups, some children showed sufficient familiarity with arithmetic facts and the long division algorithm to provide appropriate and efficient sequences of numerical responses similar to those

Table 6.2. *Solution processes characterizing observable teacher – child interactions*

Groups → (highest)	1	2	3	4	5 (lowest)
Solution processes					
Extended Precision	3	0	0	2	4
	25%			17%	40%
Precision Multiples	5	1	6	10	6
	42%	25%	43%	83%	60%
Successive Approximation	4	3	8	0	0
	33%	75%	57%		

Absolute frequencies of each observable occurrence of each solution procedure are shown in the upper portion of each row. Percentages shown below each frequency are calculated by dividing the frequency for each category by the total number of observable solutions for that group.

presented above as examples of the Precision Multiples solution. Children in all groups made some errors, however. It was the teacher's and children's efforts to resolve these errors which produced variations in the form of the problem-solving interactions across groups.

Differences in the procedural transformations across achievement groups consisted of the uneven distribution of Successive Approximation which appeared only among the higher achievers, and the relatively greater frequency of the Extended Precision form among lower achievers. Though groups had been formed primarily on the basis of arithmetic computation skills, difficulties with multiplication facts cannot entirely account for these differences in the form of the interactions. Higher achieving children were not always very accurate in their arithmetic, but they often showed a concern for monitoring the critical numerical relationships within the algorithm. One striking example was a sequence with Matt, one of the children in the highest achievement group. The following excerpt from the demonstration phase of one small group session shows that though Matt's multiplication skills were demonstrably weak, he managed to present effective goal-directed behavior as well as to *suggest* competence in multiplication, by expressing relational judgments. [The teacher writes 7)$\overline{52}$ on the blackboard for Matt to solve.]

TEACHER: Fifty-two divided by seven?
MATT: Seven times...eight?
TEACHER: ...is what? [shushes the other children] Come on, you guys. Let him try to figure it out.
MATT: [pause] It's over. [pause] Seven times six.
TEACHER: Seven times six is what?
MATT: Forty-eight...42?
TEACHER: Forty-two. Is that as close as you can get?
MATT: [shakes head "no"]
TEACHER: Can you get closer?
MATT: Uh huh. ["yes"]
TEACHER: Let's try to get closer.
MATT: ...can have six, eight times six but that's /???/
TEACHER: /It's gotta be/ times seven. It's gotta be times seven. What times seven?
TONY: It's closer to nine.
TEACHER: Seven times...6 times 7 was 42. Let's try the next highest one.
CHILD: Seven
TEACHER: What's 7 times 7?
MATT: Don't know.
TEACHER: /Forty-nine/
CHILD: /Forty-nine/
TEACHER: That's as close as you are going to get. If you go 8 times 7 is 56 and that's too big. [on the blackboard, writes in the 7 as the answer and 49 below the 52]

In spite of his difficulties with multiplication, Matt nevertheless establishes the Successive Approximations transformation. The interaction which achieves this, however, is quite different from the sequence with Jackie, presented above. Jackie had supplied numbers guided by the teacher's directives concerning relative magnitude. Here, Matt monitors relative magnitude while the teacher and other children supply most of the numbers. Matt's "It's over" establishes the "nearby simply division" goal, permitting a cooperative effort with others who shared overlapping versions of this goal. With the goal well established in the interaction, Matt's "8 times 6" is also interpreted as an erroneous variant of this search, and the teacher simply brings him back to the correct procedure.[4]

In spite of Matt's obvious difficulties with multiplication, the teacher never resorts to the full sequence of multiplication of the Extended Precision procedure. The function of the multiplication sequence in the Extended Precision procedure is not simply added practice in multiplication tables, nor is it necessarily presented as a foolproof way of doing long divisions. Its function is explicative, demonstrating important functional relationships between multiplication and division. Matt has already established the consideration of those relationships by his initial responses.

We have seen that the teacher's Extended Precision procedure embodies important relationships and constraints while drawing on routines familiar to the students. But the Extended Precision procedure cannot be taken literally as a definition of long division. It functions as a starting point or a context, specifying intermediate goals and routines from which higher order goals and new procedures which serve them are derived.

We have documented numerous instances of appropriation in these small-group sessions. When a child's actions can be interpreted as an attempt to achieve the proper goal, the teacher acts to adjust these actions by maintaining higher order constraints. The teacher's higher order goals coordinate the child's products and bring familiar background knowledge into new functional relationships: for example, multiplication becomes structured as sets of *ordered* triplets, integer multiples take on significant magnitude relationships to other integers, and so on. This results in viable long division procedures which are modified by the interpretive interaction to fit the particular characteristics of the student's background knowledge, while at the same time imposing new organizing principles on that background knowledge.

---

[4] Note also that the sequence with Jackie took place during a worksheet session in which her own written work included an erroneous subtraction, making possible further transformations of the procedure. Note that such a subtraction would not have arisen in the demonstration phase of the lesson where the teacher characteristically would not write incorrect responses. The point is that many of the seemingly incidental aspects of a setting can affect the dynamics of an interaction leading to significant differences in cognitive outcomes.

The importance of the student's actions is brought out by the cases in which students gave no products or uninterpretable ones. At these junctures, the teacher had nothing to appropriate and reverted to the Extended Precision procedure to reestablish a basis for interaction – an intermediate context based on familiar routines and goals from which to work. This move suggests that more instruction time will be required for such students. It is important to realize that this is not necessarily an error on the part of the teacher. Nevertheless, it is also important to understand that there can be many reasons for a child's failure to provide adequate feedback to the teacher. Such reasons could involve background knowledge, mental capacity, emotional problems, or matters which are social or accidental – as for example a temporary misunderstanding. In any case, without interpretable productions by the student, the teacher can only guess at the appropriate next move.

Interaction as the source of change

Our close observations of the teacher–children interactions across the five ability groups make clear that differences in outcome corresponded to different instructional interactions. What is also clear is that the differences in outcomes were not a direct result of the children's entering abilities. These abilities, specifically the prior mastery and accessibility of the multiplication facts, resulted in different instructional interactions. For some of the children, the sophisticated approximation procedure did not emerge. The same lesson plan does not translate into the same lesson in all the groups.

We have seen that the process of instruction cannot be reduced to direct transmission of knowledge, nor are creative learning processes necessarily entirely internal to individuals. Our study of division substantiates Anderson's (1982) conclusion that procedural knowledge is not acquired directly. Instruction in either declarative form – as in Anderson's study – or in procedural form – as in the present study – requires interpretive processes in which previously existing procedures participate. However, the current study shows that this interpretive work can be done interpsychologically as well as intrapsychologically.

Learning the division algorithm is an interesting case for us because the process is not at all the mechanical transmission of a mechanical procedure that it is reputed to be. In fact, the process appears to be quite creative, perhaps one of the few almost universally experienced creative experiences in elementary school. While almost all children eventually learn the algorithm, we have illustrated differences in the social process that allows the creative construction process to emerge more readily for some groups than for others.

7   How the West has won

In the division lesson discussed in Chapter 6 we showed how learning an arithmetic procedure involved social construction. The cognitive changes related to a very narrow domain that is usually thought of as procedural learning. In this chapter, we will use examples from a cycle about Native Americans to show that changes which are often thought of as developmental are also social constructions. In this case, the changes occur over a somewhat longer period of time and are closely related to the structure of classroom discourse and to the typical curriculum content of schools.

After the first lesson of the Native Americans cycle we had an interesting outcome: the group of children who represented the lower achieving part of the class could not be distinguished as such based on the scores from a test given after the lesson. However, by the end of the three-week unit, we had succeeded in *recapitulating the achievement order*: the higher achievers were once again scoring better than the lower group children. In the course of three weeks, with almost daily lessons lasting about half an hour, we had a little microcosm of failure. As in the real world, there was a disproportionate representation of children in the low group who could be identified as different from the mainstream in terms of language and culture. Our analysis of the cognitive changes that occurred during the unit involves theoretical constructs which have been dealt with as matters of ontogenetic development. However, our analysis suggests that cultural processes are involved in the changes undergone by both the high achievers and the low achievers.

What we saw happening in this educational/instructional microcosm is simple: the low-group children had to do an extra "hidden" piece of intellectual work in the course of the lessons. They acquired

114

a conceptual organization of the domain that was coherent with the one underlying the instruction and planning. In addition to undertaking the explicit task along with the high-achieving children they also undertook this "hidden task." While this extra cognitive burden itself can explain the performance of the low achievers, it appears that these children may also be impeded by a very general and pervasive feature of classroom talk exchanges. That is, both the content of the school curriculum and the classroom discourse support the same categorical structure which was the conceptual organization of our unit on Native Americans.

Description of the cycle

This cycle, conducted in the first year of the project, revolved around a social studies unit on Native Americans. Considerable effort went into preparing materials for large- and for small-group lessons and other activities. Posters were used to illustrate the way of life of a variety of Native American groups. A pocket chart was used to display the set of facts to be learned.

The planning of the cycle, which was the second one we undertook in the project, was a real contrast to the problems we had with the electricity cycle (Chapter 2). We did considerable research into the content of the unit. None of the researchers or teachers knew everything (or thought we were supposed to); all of us understood how to make good use of resources for finding out something about the domain. Our planning group chose from among a large variety of topics about American cultures prior to European contact and from a large list of possible cultural groups to focus on in the unit. At the same time that we were deciding on the specific content that would be good for both teaching and research, specific activities to engage the children in were proposed and revised and refined. We felt assured that we all had a firm common ground in the subject matter, in part because of the specific and concrete nature of the planning and in part because the planning sessions quickly became a matter of choosing among a wealth of good possibilities – winnowing down, rather than dreaming up, sessions for the children.

The *explicit task* of the unit was to master the facts in the following set, which recurred in a variety of settings:

The Diegueno people got their food by hunting and gathering; they governed themselves in bands and they moved their small families around.

The Shoshoni people got their food by hunting and gathering; they governed themselves in bands and they moved their large multi-generational families around.

The Tewa people got their food by farming; they governed themselves as tribes and they had permanent homes for their large families.

The Navaho people got their food by trading; they governed themselves as a tribe and they moved their large families around.

The Natchez people got their food by farming; they governed themselves as a state and they had permanent homes for their large families.

The Aztec people got their food by trading; they governed themselves as a state and they had permanent homes for their small families.

The facts were represented in multiple formats in the course of the unit: narratives with visual aids, same-different exercises, problem-solving, role play, question-answer sequences, workbooks. In each lesson, a chart representing all the facts was used for review. After each lesson, the children took a test: they matched the ten blanks in a different chart with a list of possible answers. The *organization of the facts* represented in the charts constituted the "*hidden task*" for some of the children in the low-achieving group.

In the first lesson, the teacher told stories about the groups of people, using line drawings as the visual aids. For each group there were three drawings illustrating their food gathering, government, and home life. The set for the Shoshoni is shown in Figure 7.1. The class discussion looked across groups at each of these three functions. For example, after telling stories about food gathering among the Diegueno, the Shoshoni and the Tewa, the teacher asked the children to look at all three pictures and to find two that were the same and one that was different. The teacher focused the discussion on the two ways of getting food: hunting and gathering in two of the pictures in contrast to the farming done by the Tewa. Each group of people and each lexical term was presented in the same way.

Figure 7.1. Three pictures of the Shoshoni illustrating their food gathering, government, and home life.

Following the 18 narratives, pictures and discussions, the teacher
filled in the answers on the review pocket chart (see Figure 7.2).
Then the children took the first test (see Figure 7.3).

We continued with the unit. In smaller groups, the children met
with their teachers, reviewed the unit chart and undertook a diversity
of activities. There were role-play situations with little figures that
exposed the crucial features of social organization and gave more
substance to the category as well as to the differences among bands,
tribes and states. There was a problem-solving situation where the
children were given a tool used for obtaining or preparing food and
the food item involved and asked to figure out how the Native
Americans might have used the two together. They engaged in lively
discussions and exhibitions of how hunters and gatherers obtained
and prepared their food. The food-getting category also involved a
lesson that tied in the children's experiences with gardening and
climates with the farming done by Natchez and the Tewa. Another

Figure 7.2. Pocket chart used in reviewing lesson content.

	GROUP	FOOD GETTING	GOVERNMENT	HOMES
 ☀	NATCHEZ	FARM c	STATE	PERMANENT LARGE c
	SHOSHONI	HUNT/ GATHER c	BAND	MOVEABLE LARGE c
	AZTEC	TRADE c	STATE c	PERMANENT SMALL
	NAVAHO c	TRADE	TRIBE	MOVEABLE LARGE
	DIEGUEN(	HUNT/ GATHER c	BAND c	MOVEABLE SMALL
	TEWA	FARM	TRIBE	PERMANENT LARGE

Figure 7.3. Test used after each lesson in the unit.

role-play situation was undertaken to enrich the children's notion of trade to include money – tokens of nonintrinsic value. The home category and the variables included in it were investigated by groups of children without a teacher present as they worked on booklets that included drawings and stories to be completed. A final large group lesson brought all of the categories and variables back together again as the children were involved in a discussion of how their lives were similar to and different from the lives of the Native American groups that they had been studying.

One child remarked, while fingering some of the manipulables, "They're all the same in their own way," which we took to indicate that she had arrived at an insight of interest about the dialectic between variability and unity that intrigues students of human culture. While the task that we were tracking in this cycle might be criticized as simple or "rote" remembering, the elaborations and transformations on the input (Mandler, 1983) that characterized the lesson activities in the cycle provided an opportunity not only to "memorize" the facts but to organize them and reflect on the facts and the organization.

Learning the organization of the facts

Our organization of the set of facts was displayed over and over by the matrix layout of the pocket chart and the six little tests given to the children during the cycle. The tests asked the children to fill in facts about the Native American cultures. The format of these tests and the pattern of results for the different groups of children show the way that the groups were working on different tasks.

For each test, each child received a test paper (like Figure 7.3, a chart with 10 blanks to fill in), an envelope with 10 answer choices (each a separate rectangle that would fit in any of the 10 blanks but with different words on them in large type), and a glue stick for putting the answers in the blanks. The test paper was an 8½ × 11 chart with four columns and six rows. Each row was labeled by the "symbol" or logo that we used to identify each of the six Native American cultures that were the focus of the unit. The first column was always labeled Name, but the last three columns were presented in varying orders, always including one labeled Food Getting, one labeled Government and one labeled Homes. We also presented the rows in varying orders. A different set of 10 blanks and 14 filled-in rectangles was created for each of the six tests.

According to field notes and interviews, the tests after the first and last large-group lessons were monitored by the teachers (so that each child's independent performance is likely to be recorded on them) and were taken seriously and with sufficient time by the children (so that each child's best performance is likely to be recorded on them). For the four tests in between, there is evidence that some groups shared answers among group members, some groups had access to the main unit chart (of a different format but from which the answers could be derived), and some children fooled around using the glue stick as lipstick, mixing contents of answer envelopes and pasting answers on in patterns relevant to other forms of play activity. Thus, we report here on the first and last tests only.

The test results

After the first large-group lesson, the number of correct answers ranged from 0 to 6. The average for the whole class was 2.73. The children from the lower ability group had a higher average, 3.0, than the children from the high-ability group, 2.5. Even though the test involved reading, and reading in the complex structure of a chart, the children from the lower ability group, based on their reading performance, scored better than the children in the high group. No individual child in the high group scored any higher than any individual in the low group and no low-group child scored any lower than any high-group child; four of the children in each group scored above the average. So it is unlikely that the higher performance of the low-ability group was a consequence of hitting upon a topic that one or two of the low-group children happened to have more extensive knowledge about.

The end test average was 6.89 correct, with the answers ranging from 0 to 10 correct. The ordering of the groups reversed back to the one predicted by the ability groups. The average for the low group was 5.25, and for the high the average was 8.2. This time, individual children in the low group did score lower than the individuals in the high group. As before, 4 of the low-group children performed above average, but at the end of the unit, 8 of the high-group children were performing above average. While both groups improved over the course of the eight days, the high group started lower and ended higher. We had succeeded in getting the regular order to reappear.

However, an examination of the test papers revealed an interesting difference between the groups that was not represented in the *quantity* of correct answers. The incorrect answers are the key. High-group children answered incorrectly *but their answers were in the correct category*. If the correct answer was "tribe", their wrong answers were "state" or "band". In startling contrast, six out of the nine low-group children showed *no constraints from the category on their incorrect answers*. If the correct answer was "tribe" their wrong answers were drawn from the whole pool – they might answer "trade" or "movable small" or "farming" or "permanent large".

After the final large-group lesson, the children in the low-achieving group turned in test papers that made it clear that they performed less well than the children in the high-achieving group. However, now an analysis of the wrong answers no longer differentiated between the low and high achievers even for the children who might be suspected of "acting up" and not "taking the test seriously." All the high-group children and all but one of the low-group children were treating the categories like categories: If the answer was supposed to be "tribe," the wrong answers were either "band" or "state".

Only one of the low-group children persisted in ignoring categories throughout the cycle, including on the final test. The other children picked up the proper categorization by the end of the unit. For the high group, category errors are not a measure of change over time in the children's performance – the high group children made no category errors, even when scoring so poorly on the first test.

Taxonomic versus relational organization

How is it that high achievers "get more" out of an instructional unit than low achievers do, that is, how do the rich get richer? Part of the answer is that apparently *the lower group children start out doing a different task*; they learn to do the same task the high-group children are doing, and, at the same time, learn the specific content in the task. In the "hidden" task, the extra one, the low-group children did very well. In the official task, the specific content, they weren't quite so good, certainly not as good as the high-group children.

The "hidden" task brings up a contrast that is a mainstay in the psychological literature. Studies of memory and lexical organization have canonized a distinction among the ways that a set of items can be represented. On the one hand, elements can be related in a story fashion, with the items developing a cohesive theme. When a domain is represented in this way, the terms that are used to describe it are: *functional*, or *thematic*, or *relational*. For example, "Dieguenos hunted rabbits and gathered acorns. Aztecs farmed with irrigation canals," would be an expression of a functional-relational-thematic representation of a subset of the cycle domain: Dieguenos + hunt and gather; Aztecs + farm. On the other hand, elements can be related in a chart-like fashion, with the items expressing hyper- and hyponymic relations. When a domain is represented this way, the terms that are used to describe it are: *taxonomic* or *categorical*. For example, Figure 7.2 and Figure 7.3 above would both be expressions of a taxonomic-categorical representation of the cycle domain.

Often, in the literature, it appears that children and people from non-Western societies represent domains in a functional-relational-thematic way and older people and those from Western technological societies represent domains in a categorical-taxonomic way (Cole & Scribner, 1973). However, a variety of recent studies suggest that something other than a "developmental" interpretation should be put on such findings. The materials used, the content domains studied, the elicitation frame the experimenter chooses – all appear to affect the conclusions one would draw about whether a group of subjects uses one type of representation or the other. In fact, the safest conclusion is probably that almost any person could rely on either form of mental representation (LCHC, 1982; 1983).

As we examine the differences in the wrong answers that the children provided on the test, we see relevance of these distinctions between concept types. First, consider the initial test: the high-group children answered with wrong answers from the right category while the low-group children's wrong answers had no such categorical interpretaion. This suggests that the high-group children were relying on the same categorical-taxonomic representation of the domain that we used for the visual aid charts and tests. We can make no such statement about the low-group children: it is not clear what representation controlled their answers. It is clear that our categories did not control them. Since the first lesson relied on narratives and pictures, it is not implausible to say that thematic-functional-relational representations accounted for their correct answers; but there is no certain lesson to be learned from their incorrect answers.

Next consider the comparison of the performance of the low-group children on the first and last test: their wrong answers were just like the high group's on the last test; the wrong answers were from the correct category; the children had changed over the course of the unit. The children developed a categorical-taxonomic representation of the domain that constrained their answer choice, and it was like the one that we presented. At the minimum we have evidence that the low-group children undertook two tasks: learning the content of the domain and learning our representation of it. Perhaps, too, the children changed from a functional-relational representation to a taxonomic-categorical one. One conclusion to draw from this sort of analysis is that the low-group children did a really excellent job because they did two pieces of intellectual work while the high-group children only did one. On the other hand, the low-group children did end up performing less well on the test, indicating that they didn't know as much about Native Americans as the high-group children.

Discourse and content support for taxonomic representations

It seems insufficient to leave the matter by stating a defense about the great amount of extra work that the lower group children did. In fact, there is good reason to believe that the "subjects" were not acting alone in the process of change – that social, interpsychological structures are related to the emergence and use of taxonomic representation. Recent work on the structure of the talk exchanges in lessons can contribute to an explanation of how the language used in classrooms promotes taxonomic representations rather than functional-relational representations. One study (Griffin & Humphrey, 1978) provides a detailed description of the treatment of children's answers in lessons. Their analysis accounts for the interactional records of lessons in a variety of classroom contexts (their own corpus from a highly successful private school, Mehan's [1979] corpus from an inner-city school, Sinclair & Coulthard's [1975] corpus from a British school).

In lessons, much of the talk occurs as a three-part exchange:

1. Teacher initiates a topic in an incomplete way, often by using a question word that leaves out a part of the substance of the statement.
2. A child or several children propose a completion of the topic, an answer.
3. Teacher disposes of the child proposal, validating its functional completion of the topic or invalidating it.

Often, the three-part sequence is called an "Initiation, Response, Evaluation" sequence or a "Question, Answer, Feedback" sequence. Griffin and Humphrey analyzed the last Teacher turn in a different way, showing the role that the turn had in constructing the content domain that the lesson addressed. Rather than seeing it primarily as an evaluation of the child speaker, they demonstrated that the third part of the sequence acts as a gatekeeper for the content of the lesson. Unless a teacher goes into a lecture format, this gate-keeping turn is about the only thing that a teacher can use to make sure that the proper information is available for learning and that improper content is removed from consideration by the lesson participants. In essence, the three parts can be seen as one assertion that is *collaboratively constructed* by the teacher and the children.

The third slot in these exchanges is accomplished in many different ways, some very simple and short (e.g. "Right!" "Not quite"), some much more complex and taking much more time. Griffin and Humphrey found clear patterns amidst the varying expressions of this third, gatekeeping, turn. As expected, a major line can be drawn between the group of ways that "correct" answers are treated and the group of ways that "incorrect answers" are treated. That is, the variants that occur in the third turn can be clearly identified in terms of polarity: Each occurs only as a positive or only as a negative. The positive variants open the gate to let correct responses into the lesson; the negative variants keep out incorrect answers.

Of interest here are the ways that wrong answers are treated. Somehow, the discourse has to remove the wrong answer and get the right answer into the lesson. In modern elementary school classrooms, as the Griffin & Humphrey (1978) analysis showed, there is an overwhelming preference for a child speaker to supply the right answer; that is, seldom does the following occur:

TEACHER: How did the Dieguenos get their food?
CHILD: They farmed.
TEACHER: No. They hunted and gathered.

Instead, one of the following techniques is used:

First, the third turn may occur *overtly* followed by a repeat of the same question usually addressing another child.. For example, the teacher can provide a simple negative (e.g., "Not quite") or an implied negative (e.g., "That was a very good try").

Alternatively, the negative evaluation in the third turn may be *covertly* accomplished. Griffin and Humphrey identified four ways teachers have of doing this: (1) Ask the same child the same question (e.g., "The Dieguenos got their food by..."). (2) Ask another child the same question (e.g., "Renee, how did they get their food?"). (3) Ask a question whose answer implies that the previous answer could not be correct (e.g., "Can you get acorns by farming?"). (4) Initiate a "side sequence" that will return to the same question. The following hypothetical exchanges illustrate this more roundabout technique:

TEACHER: What are the other ways to get food that we have been thinking about?
CHILD: Hunt and gather and uh...
TEACHER: Right, trading with money and hunting and gathering. Now they didn't have money and did they stay in one place so they could farm the land?
CHILD: No, they moved around.
TEACHER: So, if they couldn't trade and they couldn't farm, how did the Diegueno get their food?

or

TEACHER: Do you remember the picture of the women making those beautiful baskets?
CHILD: Yeah.
TEACHER: And do you remember those nets the Dieguenos had, too?
CHILD: Yeah, for catching rabbits.
TEACHER: Yeah, they hunted rabbits. How did the Diegueno get their food?

In effect, all these procedures "erase" the incorrect answer and provide a place for the correct answer to go. Classroom lessons are quite nicely designed: teachers present information content in lessons; teachers of young children seldom deliver lectures to them; the three-part units allow the teacher and the children to collaborate in constructing the information content; part of the construction team, the children, are in the lesson presumably because they don't know the information that they are collaborating to construct, so they make mistakes; the three-part unit has a built-in repair procedure in the teacher's last turn so that incorrect information can be replaced with the right answers.

Education is not merely constructing lessons; it is also children mastering content. Within the lessons which, like our Native American Indian cycle, are organized taxonomically, the chances that a child will come up with the correct answer after a wrong answer has been offered are related to the kind of domain representation the child is working with. In the case of the children from the high-achievement group who shared our taxonomical-categorical representation of the domain, any treatment of the wrong answer "farming" would leave them with a 50–50 chance of being right with their next proposal. There were only three alternatives in the category, and their responses were constrained by the category, so they only had two left to choose between after one mistake. In contrast, the children who are not working with a taxonomic representation get help to constrain their next proposal from only one of the ways used to treat an incorrect answer. If the teacher uses overt negative gatekeeping, children like those in our low group have nine possible answers left to choose among in our Native American cycle. The chances of being correct on a next proposal to replace the wrong answer are quite slim. If the teacher uses anything but the side-sequence treatment of a wrong answer, the discourse gives children working with a categorical representation an advantage over the children working with some other representation of the domain.

The side sequence treatment of an incorrect answer does not reverse the situation, but it can even things up, giving a chance to children who are not relying on constraints from a categorical organization of the domain. It provides the opportunity for the teacher to provide more constraints on the answer choice than the domain representation does. As the teacher inserts a few more three-part units and builds with the child a little extra information, it may appear that the group is "off-topic." However, when the sequence ends back where it started, the extra talk can be seen as adding more constraints to the answer choice of the initial question. Considering a child's next proposed answer for the original question, the chances for it being a correct answer are increased.

Griffin & Humphrey (1978) provide frequency of occurrence data for their corpus which shows that the side sequence – the one move that is evenly supportive of the high and low achievers – is quite rare. *One answer to how the rich get richer in classrooms appears to be that the discourse of lessons gives them extra support.* In order to work effectively in the classroom on this sort of a domain, it makes sense for the low-achieving children to switch to a taxonomic-categorical organizational structure by the end of the unit.

A set of questions is raised by the preceding observed preference of classroom discourse for taxonomical representations of a domain: if the information content of a unit of lessons is represented with a functional-relational organizational structure, would our low-achieving children who appeared to start out with such an organizational structure maintain their advantage throughout the whole unit? And would the high-achieving children demonstrate the ability to switch the organizational structures that constrained their answers? And would the language used in the classroom show a marked preference for the side sequence treatment of wrong answers as the technique that supports a nontaxonomic representation?

We attempted to find a topic for a cycle that would provide us with the appropriate test case. We wanted to design a cycle where a taxonomic representation might be devised, but where it would be clearly inferior to a functional-relational organization of the domain that the unit teaching would support. Whichever topic we investigated, it turned out wrong. Menu planning, for instance, turned into the categories known as the seven basic food groups. Kinship systems in anthropology may have fit the bill, but couldn't be rationalized as educationally relevant in the classroom.

As the search continued, it became more clear that the topics in education are more suited to taxonomic representation. The topics, the discourse structure and our high-achieving children all favor that mode of organization. While we could not find the test case to answer our questions, we found instead the same difficulty that the low-achieving children found in our cycle of lessons: *what our society considers appropriate for education does not favor a functional-relational organization of domains.*

Mismatches, structuring schools and cultural amplifiers

In this work we found a way in which psychological categories, language-use structures, educational-achievement discrepancies and curriculum content could be related. We have not arrived at a clear answer about how this integration can be used to ameliorate the situation. However, an important lesson that can be drawn from these relations is that presumed "developmental" shifts between thematic and categorical organization of domains appear to be closely tied to the way our society organizes schooling. The line between what might be considered development and what might be considered learning has been blurred in a way we believe is necessary and in a way we believe necessitates a fresh approach to what we call "cognitive change."

The experiences with this unit also allow us to reflect on various hypotheses about educational failure, specifically the "match–mismatch" and "structuring schools' efforts referred to in the first chapter. Since we recreated in microcosm the failure that occasioned the theories, we should be able to make some headway by examining our unhappy accomplishment. It looks like this cycle gives us good reason to say that both accounts are right. The high-group children "matched" the representation of the domain that the lessons and tests expected, while the low-group children experienced a "mismatch." The mismatched group eventually suffered educationally. But it also appears that the structuring of talk-exchanges in classroom lessons supports the way the high group starts out more than it supports the low achievers' approach. However, both accounts run into difficulties: Why did the mismatch matter over the three-week period of the Native American unit but did not matter for the first lesson? How is it that the same talk structure functions in two different ways – structuring success for some and failure for others?

Rather than suggest that subtle interactions of "mismatches" and "structuring" should be investigated in future research, we add a third term to derive a different viewpoint to guide our efforts. The term "cultural amplifiers" has been used to refer to intellectual tools like written language (Bruner, 1966). Here, we want to note that the various entities studied under the "mismatch" and "structuring" hypotheses can be thought of in a unified way as cultural amplifiers. Furthermore, cultural amplifiers hint at the fact that the process of change can be investigated by going beyond the processes internal to an individual. Elsewhere (Cole & Griffin, 1980) we have pointed out that cultural tools work only when they are picked up and used; that is, just because the amplifiers exist or because a person has one available and has learned how to use it, there can be no uniform expectation that an effect from the amplifier will be found, unless the occasion examined for effects is an occasion of use. Here, we want to consider what is amplified, what the amplifiers are, and who picks up and uses these cultural amplifiers.

What there is to be amplified is the children's ability to get to know some things about Native Americans. A second-level amplification could also operate: if the children are using a taxonomic or thematic representation to amplify their ability, then that amplifier could itself be amplified. The potential amplifiers in this case are written re-presentations of the domain in categorical form, pictorial representa-tions of parts of the domain in thematic form, internal underlying representations in categorical and thematic forms, talk and action sequences between teachers and children that co-construct the domain, policies and values that pick out certain domains for inclu-sion in educational contexts, and, indeed, the provision of an educa-tional system altogether.

Starting at the end of the list, we can say that the educational system as amplifier is picked up and used by parents, children and the whole society, even with the force of law behind it. The agent behind the forces that lead to inclusion of some domains and exclusion of others in education is more diffuse: historical events (including estimates of the future course of events) and a wide range of cultural institutions can be implicated. As we mentioned above, categorical representations are very likely to be implicated in the curriculum content chosen for educational contexts. We, the researchers and the teachers, found, created, picked up, used and littered the classroom scene with cultural amplifiers. As part and product of the educational system, affected by its policies and values, we used categorical representations to do our research on the unit and found categorical representations among the books and people we consulted. True, we made both the categorical charts and the more thematic pictures. But the thematic representations in the pictures were subordinated in the lesson plan to a categorical one: the stories in the pictures could be used to get the children to "see" the same/different contrasts that underlay the categorical representation. The lesson plans we made assumed the kind of collaborative classroom discourse that we described above as also favoring the categorical representation.

By this time, the picture of the classroom is quite crowded with cultural amplifiers and with all the people who have picked them up for use. Now, it is time to bring in the children, and with each group of them a pressing question arises.

First, why did the high-group children do so poorly according to the quantitative scoring of the first test? Their performance not only counters predictions based on the "match" hypothesis or the "structuring" hypothesis, their performance was well below what chance guessing would account for! A reasonable answer is to say that they joined in with the planners and the teacher, getting busy "picking up" the cultural amplifiers. They approached the task of learning about Native Americans by first searching for and finding a cultural amplifier for their learning, that being a categorical representation of the domain. We may say that there were amplifiers available that enhanced their ability to find categorical representation as the best amplifier. The lesson talk, the review chart, the test paper all amplified the amplifier the test suggests they were working on. If we score their first tests on the basis of whether they "found" and used some cultural amplifier, then they all achieved a perfect score. In the rest of the lessons of the unit, the classroom discourse, the review chart and the test chart continued to amplify their amplifier. In the short run of the lesson the high-group children found a lot in the social world that amplified their effort to apply their taxonomic amplifier; in the long run, using the amplifier paid off – they succeeded in learning a great deal about Native Americans. We don't think there is anything mysterious about why these children used a taxonomic representation – the setting they entered to learn redundantly presented that amplifier. The only thing that could make this finding mysterious would be a failure to recognize the social world as an important factor in the formation of representations.

Now, for the second group, we can apply the same reasoning as we did to the high-group children. We may say that the low-group children, too, were picking up and using a cultural amplifier in the first lesson, but in their case it was thematic organization of the domain. In the segment of the lesson involving stories about pictures, they could find such representations being used and made available for them to pick up and use. In the short run, the amplification of their amplifier paid off. They remembered a bit about the Diegueno, Shoshoni, etc. However, in the long run, as the classroom discourse and the charts recurred in the same form and as the stories changed from lesson to lesson, the social world no longer amplified their particular thematic organizations. What was in the social world for them to pick up and use along with the teacher and their fellow students was the other organizational structure, and so they did. In the long run, they picked up a new primary amplifier as well as more facts about Native Americans. Again, we see nothing individual or mysterious about the children starting with a thematic representation and then, when its social standing declined, moving to the culturally amplified taxonomic one.

Our point of view is simple: we think that in the initial lesson on the topic, both modes of representation were in the social situation to be "picked up" and used by the children, but one of them was repeatedly available throughout the three weeks. If new units, new tests, new topics make only one available, then the children will "pick up" that one from the culture. If more than one is available, they might pick up and use some other one; if one of these is privileged in the amount and staying power of the support, then the children, too, will be biased about which one to use.

Cognitive changes such as those we observed in the Native American cycle arise from the children's interactions with the environment. These are like the dialectical interactions Piaget describes except that the interaction is with the culturally constructed environment, not just the universal physical properties of the environment. The apparent unidirectionality of ontogenetic sequences may have more to do with the fact that one of the poles of the interaction is carrying a big stick, backed up by centuries of cultural experience.

8 Conclusions for a cognitive science of education

We began our project in an attempt to get the "same task" to happen in different settings. Success with this attempt could give us an analytic handle for understanding how cognitive change occurs for students and teachers across a variety of settings. While we knew perfectly well that the task would never be exactly the same once we varied the social conditions, we thought that the way that different settings pulled the task apart would tell us something about the nature of the setting as a place where cognitive change can happen. What have we learned from the classroom events that we have analyzed in the previous chapters?

When we began, we accepted the standard definition of a task as a goal and the conditions for its achievement. In the combinations tasks (Chapter 3), we saw that the source of the goal was different in different settings: it was *provided* in the tutorial but it was *found* by the children in the chemicals setting. The appropriation process in the tutorial showed how a goal can emerge in the interaction – children start by working within the social constraints of the tutorial and only later come to understand the goal the tutor is trying to provide. In the chemical indicator lesson (Chapter 5), we saw that the time frame of the teacher's goals was different from the children's (and the researchers') and was different for the components of the task: in mixing chemicals, children were able to take over the task while in recording the mixtures, which was tied to a larger concern for the teacher, tighter control was maintained. In the division lessons (Chapter 6), we see a peculiar thing happening. The task set by the teacher – to find precisely a number that when multiplied by the divisor is close to but less than the dividend – is allowed to disappear and to be replaced with a method of working that uses successive approximation. In the lessons in Chapter 7, we find that the explicit goal of learning a set of facts about various Native American groups overlays the implicit cultural goal of using category schemes to organize information.

The "tasks" we created were indeed pulled apart in multiple ways. In fact, we find that our original definition of a task as a goal and the conditions for its achievement is quite inadequate in the face of this diversity. Not only do the "conditions for achieving the goal" change from situation to situation and over time in the same situation, but the goals also appear, disappear, and change. As children's actions are appropriated, the children's role in, and understanding of, the activity are modified. Furthermore, the time frames in which tasks are undertaken vary across settings and among people in the same setting; especially important is the general finding that the activity of teaching often has a very different time frame from assessment.

The crucial difficulty with the original definition of a task is that there is always more than one person to consider as soon as one moves beyond the standard analysis of a psychological experiment. Thus, there are always multiple analyses and interpretations of the task. Even the psychological experiment, for which our definition of a task was invented, contains multiple interpretations. It is just that the experiment is constructed to warrant ignoring all but the "official" interpretation (as we argue in Chapter 3). A cognitive science of education, which concerns the variety of settings in which cognitive change occurs, will have to think of tasks in a different way. We suggest that tasks are *strategic fictions* that people use as a way of negotiating an interpretation of a situation. They are used by psychologists and teachers as well as children to help organize working together. As researchers we will fail if we set out to specify "the task" or even the set of tasks in a particular situation of learning and development. What we can try to specify are the sets of understandings that are currently being negotiated as the specific task goal and constraints change in order to accommodate cognitive growth.

In spite of these findings about the interpsychological status of tasks, a cognitive science of education is not disabled. Expanding our domain from the individual learner to the changing functional systems which include multiple people and points of view opens up a theoretical perspective that can be very fruitful in tackling questions about cognitive change. The concepts we outline in Chapter 4 provide a basis for our studies of cognitive change. We take as our unit of analysis an interpsychological functional system. Within this system, some task or set of tasks is being negotiated. Roles can change as one member becomes more expert. Cultural amplifiers – written language, category schemes, computers – can be introduced to the system, again modifying the work that gets done and the way that it gets done. In the case of education, these functional systems are zones of proximal development in which children can carry out complex tasks negotiated and mediated with more expert members of the culture. *The multiple points of view within a ZPD are not seen as a problem for analysis but rather the basis for a process of appropriation in which children's understandings can play a role in the functional system.* A theory which welcomes multiple points of view also welcomes developmental discontinuities and multiple representations as a natural consequence of the social construction of knowledge. Without falling into the trap of believing that knowledge is simply transmitted from one generation to another, a theory of cognitive change can see the powerful influence of cultural knowledge. The construction of knowledge in the ZPD remains open to creative changes which build on the culture's histroy.

Our observations and analyses of activities in the laboratory and classroom settings, guided by this theoretical perspective, lead us to a set of conclusions about cognitive change and the engineering of instructional settings. We present our conclusions in the three following sections. First, we find that the process of appropriation, in which the teacher interprets the child's responses in terms of her own analysis of the task, has important consequences for how issues in research and practice can be formulated. This is especially important for children who enter the instructional sequence with understandings that are different from the norm the teacher expects. At the same time, effective appropriation may be critical for the process of transfer to settings outside of school. Second, we find that differences between teachers and researchers are unavoidable because of the profound differences between the activities of research and practice, but these differences provide a constructive basis for understanding cognitive change. Third, designing instruction for children, especially instruction which has some hope of reaching children often left behind in the educational process, must be thought of as creating systems of social interaction. In this enterprise the ZPD concept and the notion of the whole task, introduced in Chapter 3, are very useful. We concentrate especially on the application of our findings to new educational technologies.

Appropriation, multiple analyses, and multidirectional change

We have seen in our analyses many cases in which two people in interaction have different understandings of the task or situation. Multiple realities are not necessarily an occasion for miscommunication. They are a necessary part of any social encounter. Successful communication does not require the participants to have identical analyses of the situation. If that were the case, not very much communication would be needed. Rather, the limits to successful communication are constrained by the possibility of the participants appropriating each others' actions. In this section, we will begin with a consideration of how the process of appropriation reframes questions about educational problems and end with a consideration of how the same process reframes the crucial question of relating school experiences to their out-of-school use.

The appropriation process does have limits which have an important impact on both research and instruction. The educational problems facing low achievers and their teachers are intimately linked to difficulties in the process of appropriation. We will describe two kinds of problems. In one, noise in the system of interactions between a researcher and a child results in the child ending at a lower level than he began with. This case occurred during the combinations task ("movie stars" tutorial) analyzed in Chapter 3. The second case is taken from the division cycle (analyzed in Chapter 6). It will illustrate how differences in kinds of errors that children make have an effect on the kinds of appropriation a teacher can undertake.

A case of "backward" change

When it came to appropriating some children's actions and products into the interpsychological arena, the researcher/tutor occasionally failed to produce an understanding that matched the specific configuration the child created, even in the relatively controlled laboratory-like version of the tasks. The "movie star" combinations task required that the child make all the possible pairs while working with a row of small cards with movie stars' pictures on them. The experiment included a training phase in which the child was introduced to a systematic approach to combining variables as the tutor and child checked the child's work while moving sequentially across the row of cards. Some children worked from left to right across the row, instead of from right to left, but with warning beforehand and care, the researcher was able to adjust the procedure so that the child's prior actions could be appropriated to the more advanced system; most of the children could be seen to use a more advanced strategy and to "get" the goal in subsequent trials. Ricardo was a child who moved from left to right; more important, he was working in a second language, English, and using the first names of movie stars to refer to his actions. This added to the adjustments the tutor had to make; evidently it added too much for the system to handle. At the start Ricardo, himself, was a star: he was one of the few children who, on the first trial, arranged the cards in a proper intersection configuration. The researcher adjusted to his left-to-right procedure. However, when it came to the discussion after the second trial, trouble began. Two of the movie stars he was working with had names which he pronounced in a way that made it difficult for the researcher to discriminate between them when they were used out of context. His pronunciation was normal for a native Spanish speaker producing a proper noun. When Ricardo said Sean, the researcher interpreted it as John on some occasions and on others as Sean. The same variability happened with John. The verbal ordering of the pairs is very important in this tutorial because it appears to be the verbal ordering, not the physical ordering of the cards that is the key to cognitive change. With the confusion between Sean and John, the systematicity that Ricardo started with (the systematicity that the researcher hoped to amplify) simply disappeared. The researcher even lost the ability to adjust to the left-to-right ordering. Unfortunately, the ensuing confusion meant that intersection did not become part of the interpsychological context and Ricardo, on subsequent trials, did not use it again. Instead, he used a random pairing strategy for production and checking. The noise in the system that inhibited the appropriation of his actions appears to have obliterated both the goal and the advanced strategy. The "same" interactional script that appears to have successfully initiated some children into using a more developed approach to the task appears, in Ricardo's case, to have undermined his advanced beginning.

This case indicates the importance of the larger social context that cognitive change takes place in. Instructional interactions are enormously complex, providing leeway both for creative changes that go beyond what the teacher expects and changes that subvert the educator's intentions. Systems for cognition are not closed and tidy. In the potential diversity we see hope for creativity and positive change: if cognitive change were simply a direct transmission of knowledge from one generation to the next, historical changes quite simply would not be possible. When the teacher and child are engaged in instructional interaction, that is, working together in a zone of proximal development, the endpoint the child gets to is not determined by the teacher's understanding. The zone may be distorted as in the case of Ricardo. But for different children, the same teacher input may lead in many different directions.

Just as the "system" could handle the children who went from left to right, so could the tutorial and educational systems in general accommodate speakers of different languages. When language and cultural differences among the participants in a classroom become "too much," inhibiting progressive cognitive change, is difficult to specify. Currently, much effort is expended on testing children to assess whether their expertise in English is sufficient for them to survive in an all-English classroom. We doubt the wisdom and practicality of these endeavors. Ricardo was doing well enough in the English classroom and on the playground; the problem is not his lack of English; rather, the problem is the lack of resources in the system when they happen to be needed for cognitive growth.

Especially in places like southern California, where our research took place, the resources for a Spanish speaker are easily available outside the classroom – in consumer outlets and factories, for instance. To allow educational "systems" to be ready for Ricardo, the resources need to be accessible for school as well. Assessing or even "fixing" the child to fit into the environment is not the only or most plausible answer. Rather, providing an environment where the wealth of the child's experiences can be interpreted and appropriated is required. One example of the ways that resources can be made available is in the recent work of Luis Moll and Steve Diaz (1987). After-school time, university–public school cooperation, bilingual reading experiments and innovative uses of computers provide resources that can offer more opportunities for the appropriation of the actions and talk of children like Ricardo. Rather than seeing that the children have a minimum capacity to exist in an English classroom, Moll and Diaz arranged for contexts where the children meet academic tasks rich enough in resources so that the children's acts can be properly appropriated, as the children, in turn, appropriate the resources their dual cultural heritage makes available to them.

A case of failed appropriation

The second case focuses more on individual than cultural or language differences. Another kind of limit on the appropriation process can be seen most clearly in the "inappropriate" responses that children give during the instructional process. Recall the difference between Jackie and Eric in the division lesson discussed in Chapter 6. Jackie, the successful student, made an error in computation that was interpretable as a wrong answer to the task at hand. The teacher, knowing the task that Jackie was engaged in, could make an "appropriate" next move that would be of use to Jackie's growing understanding. Eric, a student in the bottom math group, wrote down an answer that was so entirely out of the teacher's ball park that the teacher had no recourse except to back up in the procedure to a point on which she had some hope of finding common ground with Eric. When the child makes a mistake on "the" task, the teacher can work with it and show the child how it is an error. When the child is *doing some task other than the one the teacher expects* the child to be working on, the teacher cannot show the child how his responses could be improved. In our terms, she cannot appropriate it to her task.

A teacher may, of course, be mistaken about the child's response: she might fail to see how it fits in (as the researcher did with Ricardo's responses in the case described above), or she may think the child's response is a part of her task when it is not. Eric, for example, might have accidentally produced an answer that had the appearance of an interpretable mistake. The teacher's appropriation of that response, however, might not be interpretable to Eric, and the interaction might eventually break down or otherwise be unsuccessful. Working such an interaction through to an ultimate success, perhaps by retreating to an earlier stage in the process to establish common ground, would require considerable concentration and individually focused effort, commodities that teachers seldom have in a classroom filled with 25 other children. Consequently, the mainstream children who are doing the task in the "appropriate" manner, receive instruction. Children like Eric receive a kind of instruction that neither they nor their teachers can build on; sooner or later, they are left behind. The teacher's alternatives for handling responses, in effect, the *teacher's* coding scheme, necessarily breaks down in the face of low-achieving children who are not doing the task as the teacher understands it.

A problem of misappropriation

Researchers attempting to code classroom processes are in precisely the same dilemma. As we report elsewhere (Griffin, Cole & Newman, 1982), standardized coding schemes appear to give a valid picture only for some of the children. In particular, they describe children who interpret the task in the same way as the teacher and researcher; many low achievers who are coded as "doing the task poorly" are in fact not doing it at all. In this sense, the coding schemes are biased toward the normative student.

In an important respect, teachers have some advantages over the researcher attempting to code the children's behavior. The teacher is not restricted to a single guess about the child's behavior. She can interact with the children in structured ways such as those we have been describing and thereby find out if her appropriation of the child's response is interpretable to the child. The researcher has no such check on the outcome of the coding. Because the coding scheme samples only a single point in time, it necessarily assumes that the behavior is uniquely analyzable, an incorrect assumption that can lead to dangerous misappropriations of children's behavior. Nor is the teacher restricted in her interpretation to a single sequence of discourse. The teacher has a longer history with each child. Throughout our work in the classroom we were continually impressed with the richness of the knowledge that a teacher builds up over the course of daily interactions with the child. This vast knowledge of individual patterns considerably increases the range of her well-grounded interpretation of the children's responses. Without this knowledge (for example, at the beginning of the year or in cases of rapid student turnover) the teacher is in a disadvantageous position similar to that of the researcher: she is far more dependent on normative expectations. Those expectations almost invariably favor the children from the mainstream and majority culture and render the other children's responses uninterpretable (or, incorrectly, "wrong").

While the danger of misappropriation is inherent in instructional interactions, appropriation is a pervasive process for positive cognitive change. As the examples throughout this volume have shown, children can learn new goals and ways of doing things when their responses are appropriated into a system of which they were not previously aware. Because the teacher interacts with the child (unlike the researcher, who simply miscodes the behavior and leaves) the child can learn retrospectively what his response means in the system as understood by the teacher.

The problem of transfer

In education there is an expectation that children should be able to identify and solve tasks when they arise in contexts outside of school. We suspect that the process of appropriation is instrumental in achieving the creativity necessary for tackling what we have called the "whole task," that is, being able both to formulate the goal and to come to a solution. For example, providing opportunities such as found in the combinations of chemicals task (Chapter 3), in which children were allowed to discover a task in the course of doing some self-motivated activity, is an important kind of experience for children to have if they are going to learn how to apply what they know to new situations. They will not learn to transfer if they are always presented with a ready-made task. A teacher's retrospective discussions are also a crucial part of that experience. For the children who did not formulate the task themselves, such discussions are an opportunity to see that a task had been potentially present in the activity.

The process of appropriation is a "stand-in" for the child's self-discovery. Just as a stand-in is used in the entertainment industry to set the lights and the camera and the sound, before the actor is ready to complete the sequence with the action, so does the interpsychological process of appropriation work with the "strategic fiction" of a coordinated task before the child discovers a task and constraints that coordinate and motivate intrapsychological action. The process of appropriation displays for the child how the task and his response to it looks from the perspective of the teacher's analysis. When the appropriation produces an effective functional system, the child can be actor, director and producer of the self-discoveries required for growing up in and out of school. We believe that appropriation is a quite general process that can account for the emergent creativity of social interactions and the growth of flexible expertise in learners.

The conflict between teaching and research

An important element in our own process of change during the course of the project resulted from the conflict between teaching and research. This was acute in our case because we were attempting to create a model functional system to observe by appropriating what was happening in the classroom. We were not just observing what naturally occurred. We wanted to make very particular cognitive tasks occur over and over. Our negotiations with the teachers provided a rich source of information about what teaching is and how the goals, resources and expectations of the two enterprises, teaching and research, differ and in many cases conflict.

In spite of the differences there was a very high level of cooperation between the two groups resulting in a mass of data being generated over the two years of the project. In case there is any doubt about the depth and consistency of the differences, however, we quote at length from an article written by one of the teachers.

[My] advocacy [for the children] was carried on simultaneously on several grounds. Research is intended to be a benefit for the children in the long run. But in the immediate circumstances, it is up to the teacher to protect the child from research situations which might violate their rights. For example, it is well-known that classroom research involves possible invasion of the subjects' privacy as well as the potential disruption of classroom activities.

All participants in this project were covered by a Protection of Human Subjects

Declaration. The criteria for protecting the rights of the children while collecting data were quite stringent. Yet knowing when a child's rights were violated remained rather ambiguous. For example, one part of the Human Subject Protection Declaration required that videotape and camera equipment remain as "unobtrusive as possible" so that regular classroom business could continue. "Unobtrusive as possible" is a difficult phrase to translate into classroom reality. I was left as the agent for the children in negotiating how equipment could be set up to be out of the way yet to obtain proper sound and camera angle for data collection purposes.

The problems I encountered were not special to this one project. They are part of a very general conflict that arises when teachers become involved in research in their own classrooms. Although it is rarely addressed openly, the first hurdle to doing classroom-based research is the difficulty in finding educators willing to participate. In principle, it should be expected that educators would be interested in keeping up with educational research because of its implications for how teaching should go on in the classroom. However, some teachers feel an unwillingness to cooperate in classroom research, afraid of work disruption, and especially of accusations of failure to keep abreast of new trends in their field. Fear of such criticism is, in fact, central to the reluctance of teachers to participate in such work.

Many teachers I know assume that educational researchers end up exposing and criticizing the practitioner and/or the educational system. It is easy to see how teachers might get this impression from the kind of research that is published about teachers and schools. Aside from curriculum research, teachers usually hear about work that shows how teachers are doing it all wrong. *Pygmalion in the Classroom* is a good example. It points out that a teacher can make or ruin a student's academic potential without even knowing how the influence was accomplished.

Why, one might ask naively, should a competent teacher worry? If everything was going alright there would be nothing to hide. This point of view really *is* naive. I am willing to admit that things go wrong in my classroom more often than I would like, as would any honest professional. And if videotape equipment recorded what was going on, it would be extremely easy to find cases which could be embarrassing.

When observers are in the classroom, especially observers who are presumed to be experts on the teaching/learning process, teachers experience an unpleasant role reversal. Under ordinary conditions, the classroom teacher is regarded as an agent of benefits for the children. She is responsible for helping them acquire the academic skills necessary for success in their everyday lives, a responsibility that extends beyond textbooks to the social organization of the classroom as well. Once a researcher enters the classroom, the teacher begins to feel her role change. The researcher is there to improve classroom effectiveness. The researcher is an advocate for the children, even if s/he does not know their names or their academic histories. The researcher's advocacy may result in recommendations for changes that stem from an evaluation of the teacher, viewed as part of "the problem," instead of as a beneficial agent.

Many educators I know are discouraged with their work, and have good reason to be. Complications with the demands of the public, bureaucratic organization, high student-teacher ratios, and other constraints all add to the stress of the teaching profession. Given the opportunity, they would like to talk about the difficulties of teaching in addition to the difficulties that face the children. Yet such conversations rarely happen as a part of the research process because to enter such a conversation is to undermine one's own authority with little hope that the risk will pay off in terms of improved classroom conditions. (Quinsaat, 1980)

On a daily basis, we found differences in working style, background knowledge and goals. The planning process for the cycles provided numerous examples where the everyday demands of the teacher's job came into conflict with that of the researchers'. To a teacher, it is not necessary to be able to specify all aspects of a lesson. It is enough to be able to find or create lessons which serve the purpose, are appropriate to the class, and are manageable. If a teacher were to work on it, s/he could spend the time figuring out the specifics of the lessons in the way that the research team needed, but it would demand a great deal more time than the competing demands of the full curriculum permit.

In actually conducting the lessons and tutorials, again we found important differences. The teachers could not help but view the tutorials as an opportunity to teach. The research team, on the other hand, viewed the tutorials as an opportune time to do some careful assessment of what the children knew. The researchers needed tutorial situations in which children were taken to the limit of their abilities in order to determine exactly the level at which they could process the information from previous lessons. One of the teachers reported that this conflict led her to understand that the idea of doing individual evaluations of her students was a luxury which she could not possibly engage in during regular classroom instruction. Given her time constraints, she certainly did not need such a precise evaluation in order to see how to go about teaching the children.

One of the basic conflicts between teachers and researchers is in the fact that, for the teacher, it is important to find ways in which children can succeed as well as possible in their academic work. Yet this was not necessarily the goal of the researchers since we were also interested in the ways and situations in which children were having difficulties with cognitive tasks. In the second year, we were working with one of the original teachers who had thought a great deal about coordinating the roles of teachers and researchers in this project. Thus, the teacher took it as her responsibility to make certain that lessons went as well as possible once the planning phase was over, no matter what the logic of the research demanded. Sometimes she would modify the lesson, using her intuitions about the needs of individual students. This complicated life for the researchers. It would have been convenient, from our viewpoint, for her lessons to be uniformly structured. They weren't, of course. But the changes eventually became part of the data (e.g., Chapter 6) since we wanted to know when the requirements of classroom goals would require changes in the cognitive demands placed upon the children. This simply alludes to the idea that research, as well as teaching, often needs to be modified as the process under observation unfolds.

The teacher's comments show us that researchers of cognitive change create very different conditions for the process of cognitive change than teachers do. First, researchers seldom have the rich knowledge of the individual child's history, capability and personality. It is easy to standardize 27 tutorials if you are unaware of the different opportunities and difficulties that each child presents. Second, in research, assessment is indispensable since without it there are no data or findings. But assessment can get in the way of teaching which is guided by strong hypotheses derived from the history of the individual child. Third, in research the future with the child is very limited; if the assessment or training does not "work" on the first try, there is not much in the way of another chance. But the teacher has the child for the rest of the day, the rest of the year, and has a pretty good idea of whether the child will get another chance in the succeeding school years; to cut off a session is different for each enterprise, since the teacher also has a future projected with/about the child and the researcher does not.

A fourth difference derives from a deep difference in the underlying motives of the two activities. In both psychology and education there is the need to get people to do tasks that they would be unlikely to confront if left on their own. In both cases an expert must interact with a novice to present the problem and to oversee the methods that are devised for solving it. But in an important sense the psychologist's job is a lot easier than the teacher's. The psychologist must move the child from not doing the task to doing it when told to do it in the laboratory. The teacher must move the child from not doing the task to doing it on his own in everyday life. The teacher must help the child to grow up. In everyday situations there is not always an expert getting the task to happen and explaining the procedures. But educators want children not only to be able to solve problems when they are told to do so in a lesson or on a test but also to "find" the problems in everyday situations (Bransford & Stein, 1984). The teacher can never know the outcome of a lesson because the consequences are expected to be felt for years afterwards when she is no longer there to test them.

We consider collaboration between practitioners and researchers to be critical for advances in educational theory. Among the many benefits we found were a deeper understanding of how the appropriation process is played out in classrooms, how children can respond when not under the constraints of laboratory tasks, and a clear sense of the goals and priorities of teachers. We do not deny that one of our central goals is to change, specifically to improve, instructional interactions. But we have to view the interactions leading to change as ones where both sides have equal claim in constructing the changes that are to result.

Designing instruction

Where we resonate most strongly with current formulations of cognitive science is in the notion of creating "artificial" systems (Simon, 1981). Research on education is also a science of the artificial: the study of how educational interactions work can never be far removed from the task of engineering them to work better. The analyses we have presented in the previous chapters have pointed to specific recommendations for designing instruction. In this section, we explore two issues which follow from our focus on interpsychological constructive processes. The first deals with the most obvious cultural amplifier in the current sociohistorical circumstances, while the second deals with what we think is the most powerful amplifier, the ZPD.

Computer-mediated instruction

Cognitive science has had a close relationship to computers because of the use of artificial intelligence as a critical topic and method for the emerging discipline. This interest has naturally extended to approaches to instruction where there is a growing interest in intelligent tutoring systems (Sleeman & Brown, 1982; Anderson, Boyle & Reiser, 1985; Wenger, 1987). Research has also been reported on intrinsic motivation in relation to computer environments (Malone, 1981).

Our own approach in the area is to emphasize the social environment of instructional materials. This contrasts with the tendency in cognitive science approaches to look at the student–machine interaction rather than seeing the machine as a mediator between the teacher and the student or the teacher as a mediator between the student and the machine. Designing more effective instruction must involve designing systems of social interaction and social organization. Better textbooks or better microcomputer "courseware" will be only as good as the multiple settings in which teachers get them to function.

Research reported by Malone (1981), for example, lists a number of features of computer games that are found to be intrinsically motivating. Features such as a clear goal and challenge were found to be attractive to children in settings where adults were not offering any encouragement or support (extrinsic motivation) for doing anything in particular. From our point of view, it is notable that whether the game allowed competition or cooperation among children or whether it was designed to be played alone was not one of the factors considered in the study. We observe that children more often than not prefer to play together, suggesting that group environments should be an important objective as many software designers already recognize. It is interesting that computer support for adult work groups has recently become an important topic in the design of computer systems for office settings (Malone et al., in press; Stefic et al., 1987).

The focus on the individual–machine interaction results in some deeper problems for Malone's analysis. Goals, in his analysis, are properties of some games and not others. In our view, goals are things that people or groups of people have. Often children will invent goals entirely different from those the software designer attempted to place in the child–computer interaction. Levin & Kareev (1980) report a delightful case in which two young boys appropriated the computer-running-a-space-game into their fantasy play, pretending it was the console of their space ship and they were space explorers who would investigate a planet (room of the house) then return to the console to transport them to another planet. Software tools, such as word processors or even computer languages, can also be appropriated to a variety of goals including instructional goals constructed between teachers and children. Focusing on the social environment can free up the software designer from attempting to build all the interactional elements into the machine.

The new domain of intelligent tutoring systems is also usually thought of in terms of constructing a stand-alone machine that will replace the teacher for instruction in its specific domain. We have tried in this book to emphasize the complexity of the teacher–child negotiation in the process of appropriation. Efforts at designing artificially intelligent instructional systems will benefit from careful analyses of how concepts emerge in the teacher–child interaction. But current computer systems are actually quite far from being able to perform the feats of sensitive interpretation performed routinely by human teachers.

A recommendation that follows from our research is that the design of intelligent tutoring systems should not attempt to replace the teacher but rather it should set the machine up as a tool that mediates between the teacher and the child. With the support of this powerful amplifier, the human teacher can still act as the adaptive expert appropriating the child's responses into the terms of the machine and helping the child to appropriate the machine as a new tool for learning. Our recommendation, however, requires that the designer of the machine be sensitive to the socially organized settings in which the machine might function in the classroom. It would not stand alone. It would be integrated into a setting in which it had a functional role.

Microcomputers have marvelous potential for helping to create what we have called functional learning environments (Newman, 1987) in classrooms and other settings for instructional interactions. Essentially these are systems of activity in which there is a goal which children can take up. These can be classroom projects which engage children in quasi-real world activities such as running a business or collecting useful scientific data. They can also be simulated environments such as those supported by video stories or software simulations. For example, the multimedia set of science materials called

"Voyage of the Mimi" created by Sam Gibbon and his colleagues at Bank Street College puts the children in the role of scientists, navigators and explorers through a combination of empathetic engagement with story characters in a TV show and active engagement with the same problems in simulations and microcomputer data-gathering tools.

Such environments, like elements of many of our cycles, are able to engage children in whole tasks because the children can appropriate the higher level goals at both an emotional and cognitive level. It is important for our analysis that these functional environments work for education because they are also functional for the teachers even though the teachers' goals are not identical to the children's. The instructional goal is for the children to master certain material, but this goal appropriates the children's engagement in the whole tasks and is therefore coordinated with the children rather than in conflict with them.

Our own recent attempts to create computer-mediated learning environments have involved microcomputer networks, both long distance and local. Children in San Diego, New York and other world locations have been linked by long distance telecommunications. Similar projects have been successfully demonstrated by Levin and his colleagues (Levin, Riel, Rowe & Boruta, 1984). For the children there is the excitement and fascination of communicating with children in distant places. For the adults involved, there is the interest in having children engaged in written communication and other forms of technological literacy. From the point of view developed in this work, there is a special bonus available in telecommunication activities: as children communicate about their activities, there is more opportunity for their actions to be appropriated anew by the adults or children they are in communication with; as they re-present events for the benefit of a distant interlocutor, there is yet another chance for self-discovery of the tasks they have been involved in. In ongoing work we have had elementary children writing mail about current events, computer adventure games, problems in programming, tricks and hints and challenges about academic computer software, as well as more children-initiated topics like breakdancing and heavy-metal music. Within a well-designed environment, adults can capitalize on these activities to promote skill development in traditional school subjects – reading, writing, arithmetic, social studies, geography, science – as well as the emphasis on problem-solving and other metacognitive skills that are coming more to vogue among educators. New twists on well-known activities are made available – not just electronic pen pals, but class newspapers that can take advantage of an international children's newswire (Riel, 1985).

In addition some new forms of activity can be generated with the telecommunication potential of computers. Real-time computer-mediated communication among children and between adults and children can be turned to advantage for educational goals. Griffin & Cole (1987) report on a series of experimental uses of the media where the children's interest in technology and expertise at oral language genres (like rapping) can be appropriated for more school-like tasks of producing compositions and written poetry. We have emphasized the value that an extensive time-frame has as the teacher assesses and instructs children; extensive modes of communication available to teachers and children may prove to be as valuable. Electronic mail (local and long distance, between familiars and strangers) and real-time computer-mediated written communication (with the same variants possible) provide more diverse communicative channels, which can be turned into effective functional systems for education.

In a recent project, Newman and his colleagues (Newman & Goldman, 1987) have created a classroom environment, called Earth Lab, in which children can use computers in the same way scientists do, to collect, collectively analyze, and communicate about data. The project is developing software for a local area network which connects up all the Apple IIe computers in a school. By simulating some of the processes of scientific communication, children are getting greater opportunity to take an active role in scientific reasoning. For example, databases are being created as class projects in which different children contribute pieces of the puzzle. The database later becomes an object of inquiry in both small groups and whole class discussion (Newman, in press). In its current implementation in a New York City elementary school, Earth Lab is serving also to mediate the cooperative work of the classroom teachers, science teacher and computer coordinator who are involved in the project. The earth science curriculum being used in the project is thus able to appropriate children's interests across a variety of school settings. In turn, children are given an opportunity to use the same computer tools in a variety of contexts including tasks of their own invention. Project research is examining the organizational effects in terms of greater collaboration and increase in small-group inquiry. Of interest are the ways that the network system is helping to provide a ZPD for both students and teachers that promotes qualitatively different instructional interactions.

The sequence of instruction in the ZPD

We believe that effective uses of the computer in education will be those where the computer contributes to a ZPD (Pea, 1987). We have seen several examples of teacher–child interaction in which the task was divided between the two participants and in which, over the course of the interaction, the child came to understand the task and to do it more competently and independently. Our conclusion from these observations concerns the tremendous flexibility that we find in the system. The ZPD is in no way a mechanical transmission of predefined task components from the teacher's role to the child's role. The appropriation process, for example, makes clear that the child's role may become reorganized during the course of interaction as it becomes more and more under the control of the teacher's interpretation of its significance.

The ZPD concept contrasts strongly with traditional notions of how cognitive change takes place. If one were to try to specify a sequence of things to do that would move a child from not knowing what the task is to being able to do the task well, the sequence might look quite different depending on which conception of change was guiding the teaching. A glaring omission in our discussion of computers as educational tools is what has become known as traditional CAI (computer-assisted instruction). The motivation for this derives from our conception of cognitive change, and may become more clear in the following comparison of the ZPD with what we characterize as the traditional alternative.

An example of what we are calling the traditional view can be found in Gagne's (1968) notion of a learning hierarchy. This is a sequence of tasks in which the transfer of training from one task to the next is maximized. For each learner the optimal sequence may be different and for any learner there may be several best sequences. Nevertheless, such sequences have important general characteristics. First, the tasks are ordered from simple or easy to complex or difficult. Second, early tasks make use of skills that are components of later tasks. Third, the learner typically masters each task before moving onto the next. This conception has little to say about teacher–child interaction since its premise is that tasks can be sufficiently broken down into component parts that any single step in the sequence can be achieved with a minimum of instruction. Teacherless computerized classrooms running "skill and drill" programs are coherent with this conception of change.

In contrast, the ZPD conception is concerned with learning a task where the breakdown into components is achieved in the social interaction rather than through a temporal sequence. The teacher and child start out doing the task together. At first, the teacher is doing most of the task and the child is playing some minor role. Gradually, the child is able to do more and more until finally he can do the task on his own. The teacher's actions in these supportive interactions have often been called "scaffolding" (Wood, Bruner & Ross, 1976; Greenfield, 1984; Palinscar, in press), suggesting a temporary support that is removed when no longer necessary. While the scaffolding metaphor implies a unilateral action supporting a preplanned architecture rather than the reciprocal appropriation we consider more characteristic of the construction zone, the notion of a social distribution of the task follows from the ZPD. There is a sequence involved in the ZPD, but it is a sequence of different divisions of labor. The task – in the sense of the *whole task* as negotiated between the teacher and child – remains the same.

The two conceptions, the traditional view and the ZPD, result in very different ways of presenting tasks to learners. In the traditional approach there is a tendency to break the work down into pieces that can be learned without reference to the forward direction of the sequence. There is no need or opportunity to understand the goal of the sequence while learning the components. Thus, there is a tendency to emphasize rote learning of lower level components. The ZPD approach has an opposite emphasis since the task that is the goal of the sequence is being accomplished interactively from the beginning. The teacher appropriates the child's contributions into her own understanding of the task. There is always an opportunity, therefore, for the child's actions to be made meaningful for the child in terms of the goal of the sequence.

The flexibility of learning within a zone extends to the sequence of tasks that defines a curriculum. The notion of a learning hierarchy as popularly interpreted implies that educators can construct a curriculum consisting of a single best sequence of tasks going from simple to complex that will optimize transfer and not leave any gaps in the skills required for later tasks. The ZPD notion, however, provides an interesting alternative to that assumption. Where a task is being carried out interactively between an expert and novice, the components that the expert takes responsibility for may be "higher level" or "lower level." The expert may take charge of the executive decisions leaving the lower level operations to the novice or, alternatively, the expert may allow the novice to make the difficult decisions and give support by handling the mundane details that might otherwise distract the novice from the higher level thinking. The latter approach has been suggested as a method for teaching writing (Bruce, Collins, Rubin & Gentner, 1982) through tasks for the student which involve ordering sentences and paragraphs. The teacher (or in recent implementations, the microcomputer) provides the sentences and the child's role is to consider the higher level text structures involving topical coherence.

Our own observations suggest that in many cases the notion of higher and lower levels may be misleading. Take, for example, learning the division algorithm, a prerequisite for which, it is commonly assumed, is mastery of the multiplication facts. As noted in Chapter 6, children in the lowest math group entered the set of division lessons with little command of the basic facts. We saw that the expert successive approximation strategy did not emerge in their interactions with the teacher. The relationship between the lack of math facts mastery and their subsequent failure to learn division is far from straightforward, however, as Chapter 6 makes clear.

Two anecdotes reveal further dimensions of this relationship. One member of the lowest group, Margaret, discovered that the multiplication tables printed on the inside cover of her notebook provided a very effective substitute for her memory of the facts. The tables were particularly effective when working on division because they were ordered by multiples allowing her to scan down the table to find the particular multiple that was "close to but not bigger than" the dividend in the question. Using the table, she was able to complete division problems. In the process, she also learned something very important about the structure and function of the multiplication tables. Another child in the same group, Mark, found the division task very difficult. One day at recess after he had been working on a seat work assignment the teacher found him crying, upset about the fact he did not know his multiplication facts. He could see the relation between doing the division algorithm and knowing the facts and, for the first time in his school career, became determined to work on memorizing the facts.

We do not want to deny that having automatized knowledge of multiplication facts helps children in learning the algorithm. We want to point out, however, that it also works the other way. Confronting the algorithm organizes and motivates the math facts. The facts and their organization are given, perhaps for the first time, a clear function. We can thus suggest that the algorithm could be used as a way to drill and practice the math facts provided that in the initial phases of working with the algorithm, written tables were made available to the children. The standard sequence of moving from math facts to long division is a necessary sequence only where the tasks are conceived of as a series of individual accomplishments. Under conditions of an expert providing support for the "lower" level components, the child may profit by a reversal in the sequence. At least, it should not automatically be assumed that failure to learn a complex algorithm indicates the need to do more rote work on the basic skills. A reordering such that the higher level actions give functioal significance to the lower level operations may be far more valuable.

By way of a last word, let us generalize that conclusion: it is only by awareness of the productive, creative grown-up that is yet to appear that educators can set about doing what needs to be done with third- and fourth-grade children; it is only by optimism about eventual payoffs that educators and scientists can deal with the conflicts in what is, by necessity, a joint endeavor; it is the "strategic fiction" nature of our tasks that allows us to organize "lower level" work so that the Ricardos and Jackies and Erics and Margarets and Marks can take up the task at higher levels.

References

Abelson, R. P. (1981). Psychological status of the script concept. *American Psychologist, 36* (7), 715–730

Anderson, J. R. (1982). Acquisition of cognitive skill. *Psychological Review, 89* (4) 369–406.

Anderson, J. R., Boyle, B. J., & Reiser, B. J. (1985). Intelligent tutoring systems. *Science, 228,* 456–461.

Anokhin, P. K. (1969). Cybernetics and the integrative activity of the brain. In M. Cole & I. Maltzman (Eds.), *Contemporary Soviet psychology* (pp. 830–856). New York: Basic Books.

Anzai, Y., & Simon, H. A. (1979). The theory of learning by doing. *Psychological Review, 56,* 124–140.

Barr, R. (1975). How children are taught to read: Grouping and pacing. *School Review, 83,* 479–498.

Bartlett, F. C. (1932). *Remembering.* London: Cambridge University Press.

Bereiter, C. (1985). Toward a solution of the learning paradox. *Review of Educational Research, 55,* 201–226.

Bransford, J. D., & Stein, B. S. (1984). *The IDEAL problem solver.* New York: W. H. Freeman & Co.

Brown, A. L., & French, L. A. (1979). The zone of potential development: Implications for intelligence testing in the year 2000. *Intelligence, 3,* 253–271.

Brown, A. L., & Ferrara, R. A. (1985). Diagnosing zones of proximal development. In J. Wertsch (Ed.), *Culture, communication, and cognition: Vygotskian perspectives.* New York: Cambridge University Press.

Bruce, B. C., Collins, A., Rubin, A. D., & Gentner, D. (1982). Three perspectives on writing. *Educational Psychologist, 17,* 131–145.

Bruce, B. C., & Newman, D. (1978). Interacting plans. *Cognitive Science, 2,* 195–233.

Bruner, J. S. (1966). On cognitive growth. In J. S. Bruner, R. R. Oliver, & P. M. Greenfield (Eds.), *Studies in cognitive growth.* New York: John Wiley & Sons.

Burton, R., & Brown, J. S. (1982). An investigation of computer coaching for informal learning activities. In D. H. Sleeman & J. S. Brown (Eds.), *Intelligent tutoring systems.* London: Academic Press.

157

Campione, J. C., Brown, A. L., Ferrara, R., & Bryant, N. R. (1984). The zone of proximal development: Implications for individual differences and learning. In B. Rogoff & J. V. Wertsch (Eds.), *Children's learning in the zone of proximal development: New directions for child development* (No. 2, pp. 45–63). San Francisco Jossey-Bass.

Cazden, C. B. (1981). Performance before competence: Assistance to child discourse in the zone of proximal development. *The Quarterly Newsletter of the Laboratory of Comparative Human Cognition, 3* (1), 5–8.

Cicourel, A. V. (1974). *Cognitive sociology.* New York: Free Press.

Cicourel, A. V., Jennings, K., Jennings, S., Leiter, K., MacKay, R., Mehan, H., & Roth, D. (1970). *Language use and school performance.* New York: Academic Press.

Clark, C. M., & Peterson, P. L. (1986). Teachers' thought processes. In M. C. Whitroch (Ed.), *Handbook of research on teaching* (3rd ed.). New York: Macmillan.

Clement, J. (1982). Students' preconceptions in elementary mechanics. *American Journal of Phsyics, 50,* 66–71.

Cole, M., & Griffin, P. (1980). Cultural amplifiers reconsidered. In D. Olson (Ed.), *Social foundations of language and thought.* New York: W. W. Norton.

Cole, M., & Griffin, P. (Eds.) (1987). *Contextual factors in education.* Madison, Wisc.: Wisconsin Center for Educational Research, University of Wisconsin.

Cole, M., Hood, L., & McDermott, R. P. (1978). *Ecological niche picking: Ecological invalidity as an axiom of experimental cognitive psychology.* San Diego: University of California & The Rockefeller University, New York.

Cole, M., & Scribner, S. (1973). Cognitive consequences of formal and informal education. *Science, 182,* 553–559.

Collins, A., Brown, J. S., & Newman, S. (in press). Cognitive apprenticeship: Teaching the craft of reading, writing, and mathematics. In L. B. Resnick (Ed.), *Cognition and instruction: Issues and agendas.* Hillsdale, NJ: Lawrence Erlbaum Associates.

Cook-Gumperz, J., & Gumperz, J. J. (1981). Communicative competence in educational practice. In L. C. Wilkinson (Ed.), *Communicating in the classroom.* New York: Academic Press.

Davydov, V. V. (1975). Psychological characteristics of the "prenumerical" period of mathematics instruction. In L. P. Steffee (Ed.), *Children's capacity of learning mathematics.* Stanford University School Mathematics Study Group.

diSessa, A. A. (1982). Unlearning Aristotilian physics: A study of knowledge-based learning. *Cognitive Science, 6,* 37–75.

Dore, J., Gearhart, M., & Newman, D. (1978). The structure of nursery school conversation. In K. Nelson (Ed.), *Children's language.* New York: Gardner.

Education Development Center (1979). *TORQUE.* Newton, MA: Author.

Emerson, C. (1983, January). Bakhtin and Vygotsky on internalization of language. *The Quarterly Newsletter of the Laboratory of Comparative Human Cognition, 5* (1), 9–13.

Feuerstein, R. (1979). *The dynamic assessment of retarded performers: The learning potential assessment device, theory, instruments, and techniques.* Baltimore: University Park Press.

Florio, S., & Walsh, M. (1980). The teacher as colleague in classroom research. In H. Trueba, B. Guthrie, & K. Au (Eds.), *Culture in the bilingual classroom: Studies in classroom ethnography.* Rowley, MA: Newbury House.

Fodor, J. (1980). On the impossibility of acquiring "more powerful" structures. In M. Piattelli-Palmarini (Ed.), *Language and learning: The debate between Jean Piaget and Noam Chomsky.* Cambridge, MA: Harvard University Press.

Frake, C. O. (1977, June). Plying frames can be dangerous: Some reflections on methodology in cognitive anthropology. *The Quarterly Newsletter of The Institute for Comparative Human Development, 1* (3), 1–7.

Gagne, R. M. (1968). Learning hierarchies. *Educational Psychologist, 6,* 1–9.

Gardner, H. (1985). *The mind's new science.* New York: Basic Books.

Gearhart, M., & Newman, D. (1980). Learning to draw a picture: The social context of an individual activity. *Discourse Processes, 3,* 169–184.

Gentner, D., & Gentner, D. R. (1983). Flowing waters or teeming crowds: Mental models of electricity. In D. Gentner & A. L. Stevens (Eds.), *Mental models.* Hillsdale, NJ: Lawrence Erlbaum Associates.

Gick, M. L., & Holyoak, K. J. (1980). Analogical problem solving. *Cognitive Psychology, 12,* 306–335.

Glaser, R. (Ed.) (1978–87). *Advances in instructional psychology,* Vols. 1–3. Hillsdale, NJ: Lawrence Erlbaum Associates.

Greenfield, P. M. (1984). A theory of the teacher in the learning activities of everyday life. In B. Rogoff & J. Lave (Eds.), *Everyday cognition: Its development in social context.* Cambridge, MA: Harvard University Press.

Greeno, J. G. (1978). A study of problem solving. In R. Glaser (Ed.), *Advances in instructional psychology* (pp. 13–75). Hillsdale, NJ: Lawrence Erlbaum Associates.

Griffin, P., & Cole, M. (1984). Current activity for the future: The Zo-ped. In B. Rogoff & J.V. Wertsch (Eds.), *Children's learning in the zone of proximal development: New directions for child development* (No. 2, pp. 45–63). San Francisco: Jossey-Bass.

⸺ (1987). New technologies, basic skills, and the underside of education: What is to be done? In J. A. Langer (Ed.), *Language, literacy, and culture: Issues of society and schooling.* Norwood, NJ: Ablex.

Griffin, P., Cole, M., & Newman, D. (1982). Locating tasks in psychology and education. *Discourse Processes, 5,* 2, 111–125.

Griffin, P., & Humphrey, F. (1978). *Task and talk at lesson time: Children's functional language and education in the early years* (Final Rep, to Carnegie Corporation). New York: Carnegie Corporation.

Hall, W. S., Cole, M., Reder, S., & Dowley, G. (1977). Variations in young children's use of language: Some effects of setting and dialect. In R. Freedle (Ed.), *Discourse production and comprehension.* Norwood, NJ: Ablex.

Heath, S. B. (1982). *Ways with words.* New York: Cambridge University Press.

Inhelder, B., & Piaget, J. (1958). *The growth of logical thinking from childhood to adolescence.* New York: Basic Books.

Istomina, Z. M. (1975, Summer). The development of voluntary memory in preschool-age children. *Soviet Psychology, 13*(4), 5–64.

Klahr, D. (Ed.) (1976). *Cognition and instruction.* Hillsdale, NJ: Lawrence Erlbaum Associates.

Laboratory of Comparative Human Cognition (1978). Cognition as a residual category in anthropology. *Annual Review of Anthropology, 7*, 51–69.

(1982). Culture and intelligence. In W. Sternberg (Ed.), *Handbook of intelligence.* New York: Cambridge University Press.

(1983). Culture and cognitive development. In W. Kessen (Ed.), *Mussen's handbook of child psychology: Vol. I. History, theory, and method* (4th ed., pp. 295–356). New York: John Wiley & Sons.

Labov, W. (1972). The logic of nonstandard English. In P. P. Giglioli (Ed.), *Language and social context.* London: Penguin Books.

Larkin, J. H., McDermott, J., Simon, D. P. & Simon, H. A. (1980). Expert and novice performance in solving physics problems. *Science, 208*, 1335–1342.

Lave, J., Murtaugh, M., & de la Rocha, O. (1984). The dialectic of arithmetic in grocery shopping. In B. Rogoff & J. Lave (Eds.), *Everyday cognition: Its development in social context* (pp. 67–94). Cambridge, MA: Harvard University Press.

Lave, J. (1988). *Cognition in practice: Mind, mathematics and culture in everyday life.* Cambridge: Cambridge University Press.

Lawler, R. W. (1981) The progressive construction of mind. *Cognitive Science, 5*, 1–30.

Leont'ev, A. N. (1981). *Problems of the development of mind.* Moscow: Progress Publishers.

Levin, J. A., Riel, M. M., Rowe, R. D., & Boruta, M. J. (1984). Muktuk meets jacuzzi: Computer networks and elementary school writers. In S. W. Freedman (Ed.), *The acquisition of written languages: Revision and response.* Hillsdale, NJ: Ablex.

Levin, J. A., & Kareev, Y. (1980, July). Problem solving in everyday situations. *The Quarterly Newsletter of the Laboratory of Comparative Human Cognition, 2*(3), 47–52.

Luria, A. R. (1932). *The nature of human conflicts: Or emotion, conflict and will.* New York: Liveright.

(1978). The development of writing in the child. In M. Cole (Ed.), *The selected writings of A. R. Luria.* White Plains, NY: Sharpe.

(1979). *The making of mind.* Cambridge, MA: Harvard University Press.

Malone, T. W. (1981). Toward a theory of intrinsic motivation. *Cognitive Science, 4*, 335–369.

Malone, T. W., Grant, K. R., Turbak, F. A., Brobst, S. A., & Cohen, M. D. (in press), Intelligent information sharing systems. *Communications of the ACM.*

Mandler, J. M. (1983). Representation. In J. H. Flavell & E. M. Markham (Eds.), *Cognitive development.* Vol. 3 of P. Mussen (Ed.), *Handbook of child psychology*. New York: John Wiley & Sons.

Markova, A. K. (1979). *The teaching and mastery of language*. White Plains, NY: Sharpe.

McDermott, R. P. (1976). *Kids make sense: An ethnographic account of the interactional management of success and failure in one first grade classroom*. Unpublished doctoral dissertation, Department of Anthropology, Stanford University.

McDermott, R. P., & Tylbor, H. (1983). On the necessity of collusion in conversation. *Text, 3* (3) 227–297.

McNair, K. (1978–79). Capturing inflight decisions: Thoughts while teaching. *Educational Research Quarterly, 3*, 26–42.

Mehan, H. (1979). *Learning lessons*. Cambridge, MA: Harvard University Press.

Moll, L. C., & Diaz, S. (1987). Change as the goal of educational research. *Anthropology and Education Quarterly, 18* (4), 300–311.

Newman, D. (1978). Ownership and permission among nursery school children. In J. Glick & K. A. Clarke-Stewart (Eds.), *The development of social understanding*. New York: Gardner.

(1987). Functional environments for microcomputers in education. In. R. D. Pea & K. Sheingold (Eds.), *Mirrors of minds: Patterns of experience in educational computing*. Norwood, NJ: Ablex.

(in press). Using social context for science teaching. In M. Gardner, J. Greeno, F. Reif & A. Schoenfeld (Eds.), *Toward a scientific practice of science education*. Hillsdale, NJ: Lawrence Erlbaum Associates.

Newman, D., & Bruce, B. C. (1986). Interpretation and manipulation in human plans. *Discourse Processes, 9*, 167–195.

Newman, D., & Goldman, S. V. (1987). Earth Lab: A local network for collaborative classroom science. *Journal of Educational Technology Systems, 15* (3), 237–247.

Newman, D., Riel, M., & Martin, L. (1983). Cultural practices and Piaget's theory: The impact of a cross-cultural research program. In D. Kuhn & J. A. Meacham (Eds.), *On the development of developmental psychology*. Basel: Karger.

Norman, D. A. (1980). Twelve issues for cognitive science. *Cognitive Science, 4* (1), 1–32.

(1983). Some observations on mental models. In D. Gentner & A. L. Stevens (Eds.), *Mental Models* (p. 10). Hillsdale, NJ: Lawrence Erlbaum Associates.

Palinscar, A. S. (in press). The role of dialogue in scaffolded instruction. *Educational Psychologist*.

Pea, R. D. (1987). Integrating human and computer intelligence. In R. D. Pea & K. Sheingold (Eds.), *Mirrors of minds: Patterns of experience in educational computing*. Norwood, NJ: Ablex.

Petitto, A. L. (1985). Division of labor: Procedural learning in teacher-led small groups. *Cognition and Instruction, 2* (3&4), 233–270.

Piaget, J. (1973). *To understand is to invent*. New York: Grossman.

Piaget, J., & Inhelder, B. (1975). *The origin of the idea of chance in children* (C. Leake, Jr., P. Burrell, & H. D. Fishbein, trans.). New York: W. W. Norton.

Piatelli-Palamarini, M. (Ed.) (1980). *Language and learning: The debate between Jean Piaget and Noam Chomsky.* Cambridge, MA: Harvard University Press.

Quinsaat, M. G. (1980). "But it's important data": Making the demands of a cognitive experiment meet the educational imperatives of the classroom. *The Quarterly Newsletter of the Laboratory of Comparative Human Cognition, 2* (3), 70–74.

Reed, S. K., Ernst, G. W., & Banerji, R. (1974). The role of analogy in transfer between similar problem states. *Cognitive Psychology, 6,* 436–450.

Resnick, L. B. (1982). Syntax and semantics in learning to subtract. In T. Carpenter, J. Moser, & T. Romberg (Eds.), *Addition and subtraction: A cognitive perspective.* Hillsdale, NJ: Erlbaum.

——— (1987a). *Education and learning to think.* Washington, DC: National Academy Press.

——— (1987b). Learning in school and out. *Educational Researcher, 16* (9), 13–20.

Resnick, L. B., & Glaser, R. (1976). Problem solving and intelligence. In L. B. Resnick (Ed.), *The nature of intelligence.* Hillsdale, NJ: Erlbaum.

Riel, M. M. (1985). The Computer Chronicles Newswire: A functional learning environment for acquiring literacy skills. *Journal of Educational Computing Research, 1* (3), 317–337.

Rogoff, B., & Lave, J. (Eds.) (1984). *Everyday cognition: Its development in social context.* Cambridge, MA: Harvard University Press.

Rogoff, B., & Wertsch, J. V. (Eds.) (1984). *Children's learning in the zone of proximal development: New directions for child development.* San Francisco: Jossey-Bass.

Rosenthal, R., & Rubin, D. N. (1980). Summarizing 345 studies of interpersonal expectancy effects. In R. Rosenthal (Ed.), *Quantitative assessment of research domains: New directions for methodology of social and behavioral sciences* (Vol. 5). San Francisco: Jossey-Bass.

Rumelhart, D. E. (1980). Schemata: The building blocks of cognition. In R. Spiro, B. Bruce, & W. Brewer (Eds.), *Theoretical issues in reading comprehension.* Hillsdale, NJ: Lawrence Erlbaum Associates.

Rumelhart, D. E., Smolensky, P., McClelland, J. L., & Hinton, G. E. (1986). Schemata and sequential thought processes in PDP models. In J. L. McClelland, D. E. Rumelhart, & the PDP Research Group, *Parallel distributed processing: Explorations in the microstructure of cognition. Vol 2: Psychological and biological models.* Cambridge, MA: The MIT Press.

Shavelson, R. J., & Stern, P. (1981). Research on teachers' pedagogical thoughts, judgments, decisions, and behavior. *Review of Educational Research, 51,* 455–498.

Simon, H. A. (1976). Discussion: Cognition and social behavior. In J. S. Carroll & J. W. Payne (Eds.), *Cognition and social behavior.* Hillsdale, NJ: Lawrence Erlbaum Associates.

——— (1980). Cognitive science: The newest science of the artificial. *Cognitive Science, 4,* 33–46.

——— (1981). *The sciences of the artificial* (2nd ed.). Cambridge, MA: MIT Press.

Sinclair, J. McH., & Coulthard, R. M. (1975). *Toward an analysis of discourse: The English used by teachers and pupils.* London: Oxford University Press.

Sleeman, D., & Brown, J. S. (Eds.) (1982). *Intelligent tutoring systems.* New York: Academic Press.

Souviney, R. (1978). *Mathmatters.* Glenview, IL: Scott Foresman.

Stefic, M., Foster, G., Bobrow, D. G., Kahn, K., Lanning, S., & Suchman, L. (1987). Beyond the chalkboard: Computer support for collaboration and problem solving in meetings. *Communications of the ACM, 30,* 32–47.

Stone, C. A., & Wertsch, J. (1984). A social interactional analysis of learning disabilities remediation. *Journal of Learning Disabilities, 17* (4), 194–199.

Tuma, D. T., & Rief, F. (Eds.) (1980). *Problem solving and education: Issues in teaching and research.* Hillsdale, NJ: Lawrence Erlbaum Associates.

Volosinov, V. N. (1973). *Marxism and the philosophy of language.* New York: Seminar Press.

Vygotsky, L. S. (1978). *Mind in society: The development of higher psychological processes* (M. Cole, V. John-Steiner, S. Scribner, & E. Souberman, Eds.). Cambridge, MA: Harvard University Press.

(1986). *Thought and language.* (A. Kozulin, Ed.) Cambridge, MA: MIT Press.

(1987). *The collected works of L. S. Vygotsky. Vol. 1: Problems of general psychology* (R. W. Rieber & A. S. Carton, Eds.). New York: Plenum Press.

Wallen, C. J. (n.d.). *The view of teaching presented in elementary education methods texts.* Unpublished manuscript, Arizona State University.

Wenger, E. (1987). *Artificial intelligence and tutoring systems: Computational and cognitive approaches to the communication of knowledge.* Los Altos, CA: Morgan Kaufmann Publishers, Inc.

Wertsch, J. V. (Ed.) (1981). *The concept of activity in Soviet psychology.* White Plains, NY: Sharpe.

(Ed.) (1985). *Culture, communications, and cognition: Vygotskian perspectives.* Cambridge: Cambridge University Press.

(1986). *Vygotsky and the social formation of mind.* Cambridge, MA: Harvard University Press.

Wiser, M., & Carey, S. (1983). When heat and temperature were one. In D. Gentner & A. L. Stevens (Eds.), *Mental models.* Hillsdale, NJ: Lawrence Erlbaum Associates.

Wood, P., Bruner, J., & Ross, G. (1976). The role of tutoring in problem-solving. *Journal of Child Psychology and Psychiatry, 17,* 89–100.

Zinchenko, V. P. (1985). Vygotsky's ideas about units for the analysis of mind. In J. V. Wertsch (Ed.), *Culture, communication, and cognition: Vygotskian perspectives.* Cambridge: Cambridge University Press.

Author index

Subject index

167